WIRING
Handbook for Toy Trains
— Traditional layout wiring —

Ray L. Plummer

KALMBACH BOOKS

Ray L. Plummer is a longtime contributor and columnist for *Classic Toy Trains* magazine. He has authored four books on toy trains including two on toy train repair.

Kalmbach Books
21027 Crossroads Circle
Waukesha, Wisconsin 53186
www.kalmbach.com/books

Published in 2008
12 11 10 09 08   1 2 3 4 5

Manufactured in Canada

Cover photo: Engine, courtesy of Jack Sommerfeld. This Lionel no. 746 4-8-4 Norfolk & Western Railway class J Northern locomotive was catalogued in 1957-1960.

Publisher's Cataloging-In-Publication Data

Plummer, Ray L.
  Wiring handbook for toy trains : traditional layout wiring / Ray L. Plummer.

    p. : ill. ; cm.

  Includes index.
  ISBN: 978-0-89778-533-4

1. Railroads--Models--Electric equipment. 2. Railroads--Models--Design and construction--Handbooks, manuals, etc. 3. Railroads--Models--Maintenance and repair--Handbooks, manuals, etc. 4. Digital control systems. I. Title.

TF197 .P58 2008
625.1/9

Introduction

Why, in this age of glitzy and sophisticated command control systems, write a new book on traditional toy train layout wiring? Because not every toy train operator is in synch with the new technology. For whatever reason, some people are more comfortable running their trains with a transformer handle and other conventional controllers than with a keypad throttle that has no Off position.

Others have collections of vintage equipment, designed to run on unfiltered, 100 proof transformer juice. While these older trains can be operated on a command control layout, they are incapable of responding to many of the sophisticated features built into these new systems. Diminishing returns quickly set in, big time.

If you're like me, maybe you get more nicks and lacerations than satisfaction from sitting on the cutting edge and just want to keep your hobby simple. Having to think two steps ahead of the train, and keep all those code numbers straight at the same time, can overtax the brain, particularly after a hard day's work. Life in the outside world is complicated enough.

There is something reassuring and powerful about grasping the handle of your ZW, pushing it forward, and watching your train respond by instantly picking up speed. The same goes for stopping. Pull the handle back, and the train comes to a halt without realistically coasting for a half-mile first. If you want a prototypically gradual deceleration, pull the handle back slowly. You remain in complete control, and your locomotive won't smash through the back wall of the roundhouse before the coasting electronics give up.

There is also the expense factor. Command control systems don't come cheap. So if you have a perfectly good transformer that powers your classic toy train satisfactorily, why would you want to convert? Make the most of what you have, and spend that extra money on other things – like more trains!

If you are undecided about whether to go with command control or not, by all means wire your layout in the traditional manner first. That way, you can get all the low-tech bugs out of the track, switches, and accessories before adding the potential for any high-tech electronic ones to show up.

Lionel's TrainMaster Command Control (TMCC) system can be installed directly over existing traditional wiring if you decide to go that route in the future. Then you will have the

Wiring and powering a toy train layout in the traditional manner can provide operators with complete control and smooth operation.

conventional system as a backup, should the electronic one go berserk or crash. MTH's Digital Command System may require a few modifications to the wiring, depending on the size and shape of the layout, but installation is also possible.

Then again, with the conventional power and wiring in place, and functioning well, you might not feel the need to convert to command control. Dick Christianson, the founding editor of *Classic Toy Trains* magazine, had just that experience when he built his sprawling display a few years ago (see Kalmbach's *Build a Better Toy Train Layout*). He was persuaded to wire it conventionally and then add Lionel's TMCC later, if he so desired. Well, the thing ran so smoothly that he never did get around to making the change. More than 300 knowledgeable visitors from two national toy train hobbyist conventions saw the layout in operation, and not one of them questioned why he wasn't using command control.

Judging by the great number of questions about conventional wiring that are regularly received by the *Classic Toy Trains* editorial staff, it is obvious that many operators remain in the old school. Estimates based on the magazine's survey research indicate that more than 60 percent of the respondents run with conventional power and wiring.

Command control isn't for everyone. This book is dedicated to those of us who prefer to run our trains in the traditional way, the way they were originally intended.

1 Basic electricity

As we begin, here are a few words about basic electricity and some of the terminology involved. This will help you understand how electrical current works, so you can interpret wiring diagrams and troubleshoot problems as they arise.

There are two types of electrical current. The first, known as direct current (DC), features a relatively steady flow of current in only one direction. It is usually expressed as flowing from positive (+) to negative (-) in a circuit.

The second type, alternating current (AC), differs in that its flow of current rapidly alternates in direction many times per second. It moves from positive to negative, negative to positive, positive to negative, negative to positive, and so on. The speed of this alternation is expressed in cycles per second, a unit of measurement also known as hertz (Hz).

Most of the electrical power distributed in the United States is alternating current, with a frequency of 60 cycles per second (60 Hz). Most household appliances and other devices, including O gauge electric trains, are designed to operate on this type of power.

O gauge trains operate on household AC electrical current.

Of course, the household AC electrical current is reduced from the relatively dangerous 115 volts that come from a wall outlet to a lower, safer level, usually less than 20 volts, when applied to electric trains. This reduction is made by a transformer.

In terms of model railroading, DC is generally used for trains in other scales, such as HO, N, and G. To operate, they require a power pack, which is essentially a transformer that also changes AC into DC.

The flow of electricity

Because the flow of electricity is unseen, for purposes of visualization, it is often compared to the flow of water. This analogy can be helpful in understanding the behavior of elementary electrical currents, but it breaks down after that. However, for the sake of initial clarity, imagine that the electricity is water, the transformer is a pump, and the wires are pipes.

Let us assume that we have an unlimited supply of water (electricity) at our disposal, although our pump (the transformer) is capable of moving only a certain amount of it in

The more a throttle is turned up, the less resistance there is to the flow.

any given time. In electrical terms, this capacity is expressed as a wattage rating. The more water (electricity) that has to be moved, the higher the pump's capacity (wattage rating of the transformer) needs to be.

Similarly, the diameter of the pipe determines how much water can be forced through it. The larger its diameter, the more water a pipe will handle without bursting. There is a direct correlation here with the size of an electrical wire – the thicker the wire, the more electricity it can handle without burning up. We measure a pipe's diameter in inches and the thickness of wire according to its gauge number. The lower the gauge number, the thicker the wire.

To further the analogy, consider the diameter of the pipe (the thickness of the wire) as an indication of the flow capacity of the system. In electrical terms, this is expressed as amperage. The pressure of the water in the system corresponds to the force of the electricity, which is expressed as voltage.

The rheostat throttle on the transformer can be compared to a faucet – you can shut it off completely, allow a little to trickle, or open it up wide to allow the full force of the water (electricity) to flow through the system. Like a faucet, the more a throttle is turned up, the less resistance there is to the flow. Electrical resistance is measured in ohms.

Lower gauge wire is thicker and can carry more current.

Electrical circuits

As electrical current flows, it makes a loop called a circuit. The circuit begins at the power source, where current leaves through one of the two wires that connect the source with the device to be electrified. Then the current enters the light bulb, motor, or other mechanism, only to return to the power source via the second wire.

The outgoing leg of the circuit is referred to as the hot or (+) side and the return leg as the ground or (-) side. The circuit must be complete for the electrical device to function. In terms of three-rail electric trains, think of the center rail as (+) and the running rails as (-).

The flow of current moving through a circuit can be intentionally interrupted with a switch on the (+) side, the (-) side, or both sides of an electrical device. A switch that interrupts only one side of a circuit is called a single-pole switch. One that interrupts both sides is called a double-pole switch. Some switches are designed to interrupt, or break, a circuit that is normally closed, while others complete, or make, a normally open circuit.

With a short circuit, the flow of current takes a shortcut to return to the power source before traversing the entire loop, thereby bypassing the electrical device it was intended to power. The energy that the electrical device should have expended still exists in the now-shortened loop but has no place to go. As a consequence, it quickly turns into heat.

There you have the rudiments of electrical theory, along with some of the basic terms used to describe the flow of electricity. We've only scratched the surface, but this is as much depth as you'll likely need to know when wiring a traditional toy train layout.

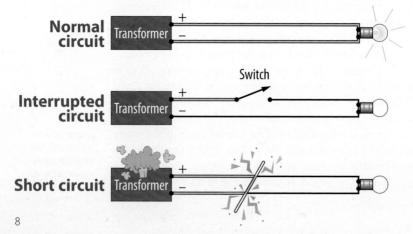

Rule number one 2

This rule should be carved in stone: Test everything before you install it on your layout.

This goes for transformers, accessories, turnouts, uncouple/unload sections, and every track section. This is particularly important when using older track and equipment, which may have acquired some unwanted gremlins along the way. Testing new pieces is also recommended.

Then test everything again as you go along – every connection, electrical circuit, run of track, UCS remote control track, and turnout immediately after you've installed it. This will isolate individual trouble spots before they become global issues and eliminate having to tear up large sections of layout later on. If you do this, it still won't guarantee a trouble-free layout, but it certainly will increase your odds. A little time spent testing at the outset will save you time, trouble, and even money down the line.

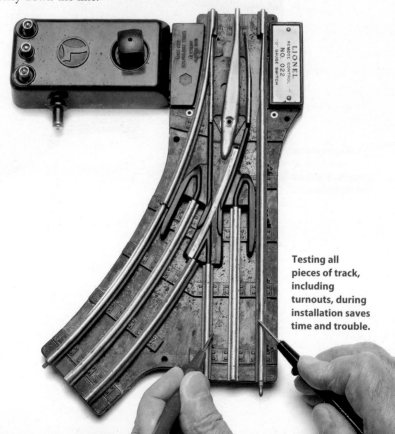

Testing all pieces of track, including turnouts, during installation saves time and trouble.

Transformers

Examine transformer line cords and plugs for signs of damage or deterioration. Next, test the circuit breakers by creating intentional short circuits across all the terminals. The breakers should kick in after only a few seconds. Then, test the outputs of the various variable-voltage throttles. They should provide smooth uninterrupted increases in voltage from their Off positions to the very top of their ranges. (For this, you will need a meter to measure voltage.) Test the whistle/horn controls to see if they work.

If the transformer fails any of these tests, take it to a professional for service. I do not recommend undertaking your own transformer repair, even if you are fearless and think you know what you are doing.

Always check transformer cords for damage before operation.

Track sections

Don't laugh. The fiber center rail insulation
has been known to fail (or worse yet, leak) over
time. Test each track section to make sure there is
no continuity between the center rail and the outer
running rails.

If the track section has an insulated running
rail for accessory activation, test that rail against
the other running rail. Again, there should be no
continuity.

Turnouts

Test each turnout and controller in isolation, with
the fixed voltage you intend to use on the layout
(18-20 volts is suggested). Make sure the swivel rails
snap smartly and lock into both positions as they
should. The controller lights should burn brightly in
both positions.

Then, test the non-derailing feature by sequentially
grounding the insulated control rails for both routes to an
uninsulated running rail. If the turnout doesn't perform well
after repeated attempts, take it to the workbench. It may only
need a little cleaning and lubrication.

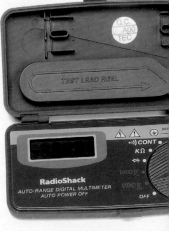

For optimal
performance,
even track
sections should
be checked
for electrical
leakage.

UCS remote control tracks

These remote control sections have two basic functions –
uncouple and unload. Hook them up to their intended
controllers and test both functions in isolation first. Often
the insulation on the four-conductor control cable fails with
age and causes unusual malfunctions. If it does, rewire the
controller.

Accessories

Test each accessory function in isolation using the controller
you intend to install. Put the unit through its paces several
times to ascertain whether it works up to specifications and
expectations.

3 Transformers

Inside every transformer there are two coils of wire, designated as the primary coil and the secondary coil, wound around an iron core. In most cases, the core is a stack of thin metal plates.

A transformer operates on an electromagnetic principle known as induction. A strong magnetic field in the primary coil induces a weaker field in the secondary coil. When 115 volts of alternating house current is fed into the primary coil, the induced current in the secondary coil will also alternate but at a lower voltage.

The amount of voltage reduction is determined by the size of the wire and the number of windings in each coil. In practice, the primary coil will have many windings of small diameter wire, while the secondary coil will have fewer windings of larger diameter wire.

With toy train transformers, the goal is to create a primary to secondary ratio that will reduce the 115-volt house current to a safe level for train operation, usually 18 to 20 volts.

To regulate train speed, the transformer has a throttle control in the form of a wiper arm or roller that sweeps across the windings of the secondary coil. It can be manually adjusted to provide track voltage from zero to the 18- to 20-volt maximum output of the secondary coil.

Many larger transformers have more than one throttle arm wiping across the same secondary coil to provide independent circuits for multiple train control. Additional taps at various points on the coil provide specific fixed voltages for accessory operation.

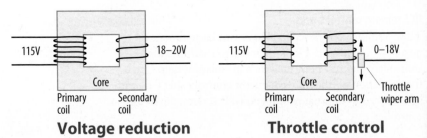

Voltage reduction   **Throttle control**

Available in many sizes and shapes, there is a transformer for any type of toy train or track.

Types of transformers

Lionel and other train manufacturers made transformers in huge quantities and in a variety of types and styles. They were all designed to do essentially the same thing and are considered to be virtually interchangeable. But the transformers made by Gilbert American Flyer and Marx had slightly lower output voltages, which resulted in a slower maximum train speed.

Transformers have traditionally been classified according to their wattage ratings, which range from 25 to 400. The wattage rating is a measure of the maximum amount of electricity a transformer can draw from household power lines without overheating. More practically put, it is an indication

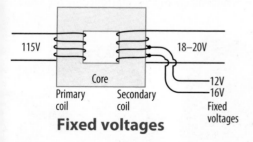

115V

18–20V

12V
16V

Core

Primary coil

Secondary coil

Fixed voltages

Fixed voltages

Large transformers, such as this Z-4000 by MTH, usually have two throttles for multiple train operation.

of a transformer's capacity to run trains, handle accessories, and illuminate light bulbs at the same time. Generally, bigger is better. The higher a transformer's wattage rating, the more you can efficiently operate with it.

Another way of classifying transformers is according to the number of throttles and/or binding post terminals they have. There is a great variety among the models.

Small transformers (under 150 watts) and a few of the larger ones have only one throttle and are intended to run just one train and a few accessories.

Single-throttle models with two binding posts are easy to classify: two binding posts mean two wires go to the track.

Transformers with three binding posts usually provide two different variable track voltage ranges controlled by the same throttle.

Small transformers, those under 150 watts, are most efficient running one train and a few accessories.

Models with four or more terminals and only one throttle offer different variable track voltage ranges, along with fixed voltages to power accessories. These voltage values usually are indicated on the nameplate or the case of the transformer.

Large transformers (150 watts or more) customarily have more than one throttle. For example, Lionel's KW model features two throttles, and the top-of-the-line ZW has four. These independent throttle controls each have their own set of terminals and can be hooked up as if they were separate transformers. When using a ZW, you can achieve fixed voltages by setting one or more of the throttles in advance.

Transformer capacity

Lionel used to advise customers to buy a large transformer from the start so that when their layouts expanded there was enough reserve energy available to handle the growth. That advice still holds true.

That is why the 275-watt ZW, Lionel's biggest and best postwar transformer, remains popular with layout builders today. It can easily handle a couple of medium-sized trains and a reasonable number of accessories – probably as much equipment as most people will ever run on a layout.

But the notion that one super-power transformer can run everything – that it can operate four trains and as many lights and accessories that can be strung together – is simply not realistic. Even large transformers will heat up and overload quickly when taxed to capacity.

At 275 watts, Lionel's ZW transformer remains a popular choice for operators wishing to run several trains.

Although the ZW has four variable throttles to power four independent circuits and is listed at 275 total watts, it can deliver only 180 watts continuously at 14 amps. The wattage is divided among the number of throttles in use. One throttle operating alone has access to the full 180 watts available. Two operating throttles will have only 90 watts each. With all four throttles in use, the number drops to 45 watts of continuous power available per throttle.

According to estimates published by Lionel in the post-war era, a single-motor locomotive draws between 25 and 30 watts. Add 10 watts for a whistle and 5 more for a smoke generator. Automatic and operating accessories consume between 10 and 25 watts each. Even the lowly light bulb can take 5 watts of power.

So you can see that the wattage draw adds up fast. A dual-motor diesel, pulling four lighted aluminum passenger cars will probably consume 90 to 100 watts by itself. That doesn't leave much for another train and a string of lights and accessories.

The amount of usable wattage available at the output is inversely proportional to the amount of amperage being drawn by everything – trains, lights, and accessories – connected to the transformer at a given point in time.

From the pages of the Lionel Service Manual, here are the usable wattage specifications for some of the most popular postwar transformers. The amperage figures represent the maximum draw available before the circuit breakers kick in.

Type	Input rating	Usable wattage at output
ZW	275 watts	180 at 14 amps
Z	250 watts	180 at 14 amps
KW	190 watts	140 at 10 amps
VW	150 watts	110 at 8 amps
V	150 watts	110 at 8 amps
LW	125 watts	75 at 5-6 amps
RW	110 watts	70 at 5-6 amps
1033	90 watts	60 at 5 amps

While modern trains with can-motor technology are more electrically efficient and consume less power than the old postwar models, it is only a matter of degree. The same guidelines and caveats apply.

Power connections for older model Lionel transformers

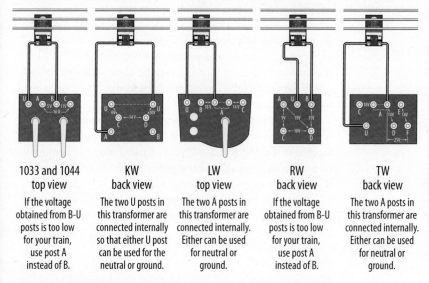

1033 and 1044 top view	KW back view	LW top view	RW back view	TW back view
If the voltage obtained from B-U posts is too low for your train, use post A instead of B.	The two U posts in this transformer are connected internally so that either U post can be used for the neutral or ground.	The two A posts in this transformer are connected internally. Either can be used for neutral or ground.	If the voltage obtained from B-U posts is too low for your train, use post A instead of B.	The two A posts in this transformer are connected internally. Either can be used for neutral or ground.

Using an older transformer

Do you need a new transformer or can you use an older one to power your pike? This is often more a question of economics than electronics. New models are crammed with state-of-the-art features, but they are expensive. Most transformers made by Lionel and Gilbert American Flyer during the postwar era, particularly the larger ones, were very well made. If they have been stored properly, they are usually still serviceable.

But before you do anything with an old transformer, check it over carefully. Start by looking for visible signs of scorching, discoloration, or disfigurement on the transformer case. This usually indicates that the unit was severely overheated at some point and probably shouldn't be trusted.

Next, make sure the plug and line cord are firmly attached. Determine that the insulation on the cord is intact, with no bare spots or cracks showing. Bend and twist the cord; it should be supple and not stiff.

Then check to see that all the binding post terminals, or studs, are tightly seated. Work each of the handles, levers, and knobs. They should move freely and quietly without binding or sticking. The buttons should spring back when you release them.

If your transformer passes this preliminary inspection, go ahead and plug it in. You should hear a slight audible hum or buzz – that's normal. Leave it on for an hour – it should be mildly warm to the touch but not hot.

Now attach a short wire to the common, or ground, binding post terminal (on Lionel transformers, this is usually labeled U and Base Post on American Flyer units). Turn the throttle to the Off position. Carefully touch the other end of the wire to the second variable-voltage terminal. Nothing should happen. Then turn the throttle about halfway up and touch the wire to the second terminal again. If you see a spark, the transformer is working.

If your transformer flunks any of these inspections or tests, turn it over to a qualified technician for service or replace it. Taking the transformer apart for any reason is not recommended because of the potential shock or fire hazard if you touch something wrong or don't get it back together right. It is far better to take your transformer to someone knowledgeable who has the tools and equipment to fix it correctly.

Circuit breakers

A working circuit breaker is the main safety consideration in a transformer. Toy railroads have always been prone to accidental short circuits from derailed rolling stock or other metallic objects that somehow land on the track. When this happens, the transformer begins to overheat. If it is not protected by a circuit breaker, the transformer will burn out.

There are two basic types of circuit breakers in common use. Type A has a very positive action. When it senses overheating in the circuit, a spring loaded breaker pops open. It has to be reset manually each time.

Type B is far more common. It too is a thermal device, but it works automatically. Sensing the overload or short circuit a few seconds after it occurs, the breaker opens. The breaker then closes automatically, but it will immediately reopen if the short circuit still exists. This sequence continues until the condition is corrected. Some circuit breakers have blinking red lights connected to them.

Using a transformer with a functioning circuit breaker is a top priority. When in doubt, have a professional check it for you, and make adjustments if needed. It takes only a few minutes. The alternative could be a smoky disaster.

Most of the Lionel and American Flyer transformers rated at 50 to 75 watts and higher have circuit breakers. However, many of the smaller models that were packed with low-end sets do not. The same holds true for many of the older transformers, particularly those made before 1940.

Using fuses

Some hobbyists use in-line fuses, usually rated at about 5 amps, between the transformer and the track to compensate for the absence of circuit breakers. While this system works, it isn't recommended. First of all, replacing fuses every time a wheel jumps the track can get expensive. Second, repeatedly replacing fuses may later tempt you to simply bypass the fuse holders, say, if you should run out of fuses in the middle of a hot operating session.

Using in-line fuses alone to protect a transformer is not highly recommended.

The only recommended use for such fuses would be as a backup system in case the breakers malfunction, and that rarely happens.

Not sure if your transformer has a breaker or not? Might I suggest the axiom: "When in doubt, throw it out."

Phasing transformers

Whenever you use two or more transformers on the same layout, they must be in phase with each other. Most of the newer large transformers – those with one-way plugs on their cords – are designed to be in phase with each other. However, the older models were not, so they can cause problems if you don't put them into phase yourself.

This means plugging all the two-pronged transformer cords into electrical outlets in the same way. Correct phasing ensures that trains pass smoothly from one insulated block to another. Incorrect phasing of the transformers causes locomotives to balk, arc, or stall between blocks. It can also cause some accessories to operate badly or short out.

How can you be sure all the transformers are in phase? Because phasing involves several transformer cords, it is best to plug them all into a multiple-outlet power strip equipped with a master switch and a built-in circuit breaker. That way all the plugs can remain inserted the correct way once they are put into phase with each other. The master switch can then be used to turn all of the transformers on and off at the same time. The circuit breaker provides additional overload protection; you really can't be too careful.

Phasing

To phase the transformers, start by connecting all the ground terminals together with heavy wire. Some transformers have a designated or recommended ground terminal, but most of the smaller ones do not (see the chart on page 33).

Check carefully to see whether the binding posts are marked in some way or not. If they are not, you can use any terminal as the ground as long as you are consistent among all the transformers in the system. (In the illustration, the left-hand binding posts on each transformer serve as the common ground and running-rail connections.)

Once you have linked all the grounds together, plug all the transformer cords into the power strip, plug the strip into a 115-volt wall outlet, and switch it on. Turn all the transformer speed control levers about half way up. Then connect a wire to the other binding post of the first transformer (the right-hand terminal in the illustration), and gently touch the wire to the same post on the second transformer. If a spark is produced when they touch, reverse the plug on the second transformer by rotating it 180 degrees in the power strip outlet. Touch the second post with the wire again. If no spark appears, you know the second transformer is in phase with the first. Repeat this operation with the remaining transformers. Then, your transformers will be in phase and ready to go.

Phasing transformers

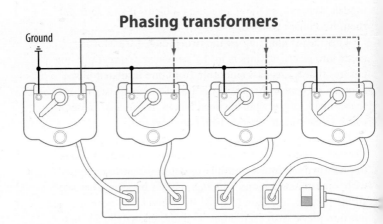

Electro-mechanical devices 4

Electro-mechanical devices such as electromagnets, relays, and solenoids were widely used by toy train manufacturers. While not specifically tied to layout wiring, a short treatment of these devices seems in order.

An electromagnet is simply an iron core with a coil of wire wrapped around it. As electricity is sent through the coil, the electromagnet either attracts or repels other ferrous metals. When the electricity is turned off, the flow of magnetic energy, known as flux, ceases. The direction of the flux, whether the electromagnet attracts or repels, is a function of the way in which the coil is wrapped around the iron core.

The strength of the magnetism, or flux density, is determined by the size of the core as well as the size of the wire used and/or the number of windings in the coil. Generally, the larger the core surface and the more windings on it, the more powerful the magnet.

Lionel used electromagnets in its uncoupling tracks since the 1940s. They may also be found in the various magnet crane accessories the company has produced over the years.

A relay is nothing more than an electromagnet that has a movable iron armature attached to it, usually by a pivot at one end. One or more electrical contacts are attached to the pivoting armature. Whenever the electromagnet is energized, the armature is attracted to it, and the contacts either make or break their electrical circuits. As the electromagnet is shut

Relays (left), solenoids, and electromagnets are commonly found in toy trains, track, and accessories.

off, the armature returns to its normal rest position, usually by spring pressure or by the force of gravity.

The most common relays encountered in the toy train world are those used to activate Lionel's built-in whistles and horns. They are also found in automatic train control systems (see chapters 12 and 13).

A solenoid is a close cousin to the electromagnet. The main differences are that a solenoid's coil is wrapped around a hollow, nonmagnetic tube and the iron core is movable within that tube. This movable core is referred to as a plunger or armature.

When electricity is sent through the coil, the plunger is made to move in either direction, depending upon how the coil is wound. Typically, solenoids are set up so that gravity or a spring returns the plunger to its normal rest position when the electricity is turned off.

Lionel used the solenoid principle in its famous sequence-reversing units, found in almost all locomotives made from the 1930s to the 1990s. Solenoids were also in the activating mechanisms of the company's most popular cars and accessories, including the milk car and the gateman.

A double solenoid has two coils of wire, wound in opposition to each other, around the same tube. Selectively energizing one coil or the other can make the plunger move in both directions. Double solenoids have been used for generations to change the position of the swivel rails on automatic track turnouts.

A relay such as this is used to operate Lionel's built-in whistles and horns.

Switches 5

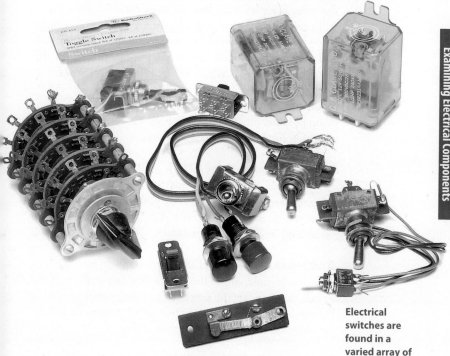

Electrical switches are found in a varied array of configurations.

Electrical switches come in many different types, styles, and contact configurations. Switch contacts are referred to as poles.

While most switches are thrown manually, a few are designed to work automatically. They all perform the same functions. Most switches are made to form permanent connections when thrown. However, there are some applications where only a temporary contact is indicated; for example, when changing the position of automatic turnouts or when uncoupling and unloading cars. Switches designed for this purpose are usually spring-loaded and are designated as momentary contact switches.

The most basic single-throw switches simply make or break an electrical circuit. Those that make a circuit are normally open, and those that break a circuit are normally closed.

More complex multiple-throw switches direct the electrical current along two or more different paths. Some can handle more than one circuit with the same throw.

There is a seemingly limitless variety of pole configurations on switches available in electrical supply and consumer electronics stores. As your knowledge grows, you may want to try the more complex ones. But the most common ones that you will encounter when wiring a layout are single-pole, single-throw; single-pole, double-throw; double-pole, single-throw; and double-pole, double-throw. They are designated by the electrical industry as SPST, SPDT, DPST, and DPDT.

Single-pole, single-throw (SPST)

A single-pole, single-throw is a basic On/Off switch, having provision on its base to attach two wires.

Single-pole, double-throw (SPDT)

A single-pole, double-throw switch is used to direct the current along one of two separate paths. Some have an Off position between the two poles. A SPDT switch has provision on its base to attach three wires.

Double-pole, single-throw (DPST)

The double-pole, single-throw switch is essentially an On/Off switch that handles the power from two separate circuits at the same time. It is like using two SPST switches and has provision on its base to attach four wires.

Double-pole, double-throw (DPDT)

A double-pole, double-throw switch is used to direct current from two separate circuits along two of four different paths at the same time. Some have an Off position between the poles. It has provision on its base to attach six wires. DPDT switches can be used in place of DPST switches, which are not as readily available.

Switch types

Although there are many variations in size, capacity, and outward appearance, there are only five basic types of manually operated switches: knife, toggle, slide, push-button, and rotary.

Knife switches consist of a pivoted blade, with a handle on it, that slips into a slotted contact pole. The action is positive and obvious, and the position of the blade can easily be determined visually. Very few knife switches remain, as they have been out of common use for at least 50 years because of safety issues (the exposed surfaces pose a potential shock hazard).

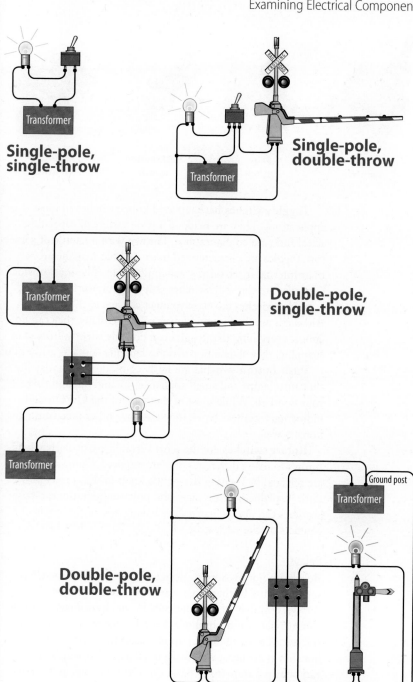

Single-pole, single-throw

Single-pole, double-throw

Double-pole, single-throw

Double-pole, double-throw

Ground post

Ground post

25

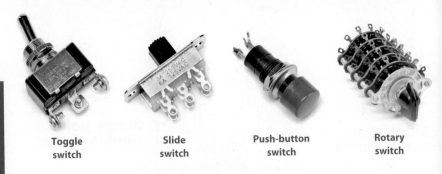

Toggle
switch

Slide
switch

Push-button
switch

Rotary
switch

Toggle switches have replaced knife switches in most applications. They are made in a wide variety of capacities, sizes, and pole configurations. Thrown with a handle of some sort, toggles are characterized by an audible snap, heard as their internal mechanisms switch positions. The most obvious examples are the wall switches that turn on overhead lights.

Slide switches are close younger cousins to the toggles. Although usually found in lower voltage circuits, they can do almost everything that toggles can do, only silently. Instead of snapping, they slide into position, changing contacts as they do.

Push-button switches are fairly common in everyday life – they turn lamps and small appliances on and off, and ring your doorbell. While most of them are of the On/Off and momentary-contact types, they can have other pole configurations as well.

Rotary switches are the most versatile, particularly where throws to many different poles are required. Contact poles are selected by rotating the switch knob to the correct position. Available in many sizes and pole configurations, rotary switches can also be ganged, by having two or more sets of contacts on the same axis.

Relays

Relays are not mysterious devices, although some modelers seem to think of them that way. They are simply switches thrown remotely or automatically by an electromagnet. Most commercial or industrial relays on the market are double-throw, designed to direct current along two separate paths, but they don't necessarily have to be used that way. They can be wired to perform basic On/Off functions quite easily. There is a wide selection in the number and configuration of poles available: double-, triple-, and quadruple-pole relays are common.

SPDT Relay

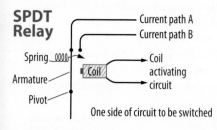

Current path A
Current path B
Spring
Coil
Armature
Coil activating circuit
Pivot
One side of circuit to be switched

Relays are simply switches thrown remotely or automatically by an electromagnet.

In its simplest SPDT form, power from one side of the electrical circuit to be switched is fed into the pivoted armature of the relay, which has a pair of contacts on its free end. This armature contact is held firmly against one of the pole contacts of the double-pole switch by a spring. Let's call this current path A.

When the relay coil is energized, the armature is attracted to it. As the armature moves, it breaks the contact with current path A and makes contact with the other pole of the switch, thereby directing the current down path B.

The relay will stay in this position as long as the coil is energized. When the coil energy is terminated, the spring-loading will again take over, and the current will be sent down path A.

Thermal switches

For the sake of completeness, I should mention that Lionel used rather ingenious thermal activated switches in some of its accessories over the years. Most notable were the automatic-stop stations, block signals, and other items using intermittent action, such as blinking lights or the walking beam on the oil derrick.

A thermal switch features a bimetallic contact strip with a nichrome heater coil wrapped around it. The illustration shows a thermal switch in the same circuit as a light bulb.

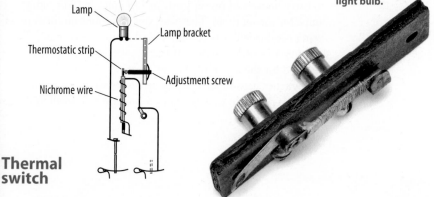

Lamp
Lamp bracket
Thermostatic strip
Adjustment screw
Nichrome wire

Thermal switch

27

These thermal switches were essentially one-function, make/break devices that consisted of a bimetallic contact strip with a nichrome heater coil wrapped around it.

Power from the circuit that activated the accessory was also fed into the heater coil at the same time. The contact at the end of the bimetallic strip and a fixed contact were both normally closed.

As the coil heated up, the bimetallic contact strip would bend away from the fixed contact and break the circuit. When the bimetallic strip cooled, it would return to the normally closed position again. Of course, this would set the heating/cooling cycle into motion once more. It would continue until the power was shut off.

These thermal switches were remarkably reliable, considering how fragile they looked. It was possible to adjust the cycle interval on some of the accessories.

Switch ratings

All electrical switches, regardless of type, are rated according to their current-carrying capacities. This is usually expressed in amperage. With the larger, industrial-grade models, this rating is usually stamped right on the switch itself. In some cases, it may be indicated on the packaging. Look for it, as this number is very important.

When using switches, as in selecting wire, bigger is better! What good is having heavy, high-current-capacity wires if all that capacity is too much for the switches in the circuit to handle? Don't make your switches the weakest link in the system. This is not the place to try saving a few dollars.

Even though most track circuits carry only 20 volts at 3 or 4 amps, it is wise to buy heavy-duty toggles that are designed to carry household power loads of 115 volts at 10 or more amps for use on them. That way, you can count on them never being overloaded or becoming pitted from excess arcing. They will never impede the flow of track power and will probably be good for the life of the layout.

Switches used in auxiliary or accessory circuits are not quite as critical. In these circuits, 5-amp switches will probably be adequate.

Wire basics 6

Wiring a layout
is made easier by
using the proper
gauge wire.

People accustomed to thinking in terms of starter sets running on ovals around the Christmas tree powered by small coils of thin wire tend to overestimate the current handling capacity of wire. When choosing wire for a permanent layout, remember two things: size matters and bigger is better.

To use our water analogy again: Just as a larger diameter pipe allows for a greater flow of water, a heavier gauge wire does the same thing for the flow of electricity. Think of wires as the arteries that deliver life to the layout.

You can't have too many track feeder wires on a large layout. There will be enough power loss in the tracks themselves – you don't need to lose even more in the wires leading up to them.

Should the wire be solid or stranded? There is probably not much difference noticeable on a toy train layout, although

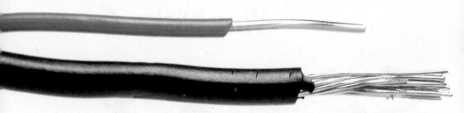

some people claim that stranded wire is a better conductor. Stranded wire is more supple and easier to handle. Solid wire might be better for power buses, which are usually attached to the benchwork in some way and will need to be stripped in odd places to attach feeders. It boils down to personal preference and availability.

All electrical wire is classified by gauge. According to American Wire Gauge (AWG), each different diameter of wire is assigned a gauge number. For some reason, these gauge numbers are just the opposite of the wire size – the smaller the AWG number, the heavier the wire.

You should use 12- to 14-gauge wire for power buses, 16-gauge minimum for track feeders, and 18- to 20-gauge for short runs to lights and accessories. Anything smaller than 20-gauge isn't of much use.

I strongly urge you to color code all wiring, consistently assigning a specific color to each application. Use one color for ground return buses, another for track power feeders, a third for fixed-voltage accessory circuits, and so on.

Buy wire in as many colors and shades as you can find. It doesn't take very long to run out of options. Different suppliers sell different color variations, so you may have to go to more than one place to meet all your requirements.

**Manufactured
in many colors,
wire can be
color coded on a
layout to keep it
organized.**

Common grounds 7

Using a common ground, also known as a common return, regardless of the kind of transformer arrangement or power source you use, is highly recommended. The reason is simple. A common ground system can expedite your wiring and save you money in the process because you'll need only about half as much wire.

Instead of using two wires to complete each electrical circuit with the transformer, you connect only one to the hot, outgoing or center-rail side of the circuit (+). The ground or return side of the circuit (-) uses a path in common with all the other circuits in the system to get back to the power source. One ground connection may be used for all track blocks, turnout motors, lights, and accessories on the layout. It doesn't matter how many circuits share the same common ground, all find their own paths back to the power source without interfering with each other. (Don't ask how; electricity just works that way.)

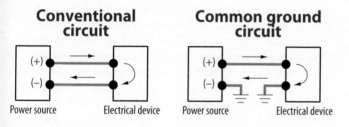

Conventional circuit

(+)
(-)

Power source   Electrical device

Common ground circuit

(+)
(-)

Power source   Electrical device

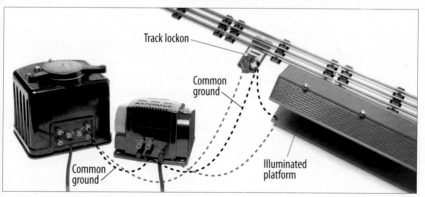

Track lockon

Common ground

Common ground

Illuminated platform

Wiring a common ground

A common ground wiring system is efficient and eliminates excess wire.

Many operators find it convenient to use the track running rails as common ground connections for all the electrical circuits on their layouts. This is an efficient method for small and medium-sized model railroads. On large ones, however, with their long stretches of track and numerous lights and accessories that drain away power, it is recommended that all the ground leads be connected to a heavy copper wire running underneath the layout. Electricians call such a thick wire a bus. These ground bus wires are usually installed around the periphery of the layout or cut across it diagonally. That puts them in close proximity to the track and the accessory circuits they serve.

Large Lionel transformers, particularly those with several control circuits, often have common ground terminals that have been connected internally to simplify wiring. If your transformer doesn't have these terminals, or if you aren't sure if it does, consult the following chart. It shows the various circuit combinations available on many of the popular postwar Lionel models and should help you select a workable common ground terminal.

Transformer terminals used for common ground wiring

Transformer	Common or ground post	Fixed-voltage posts	Variable voltage posts
KW multi-control	U	D 20 V C 6 V	A 6-20 V B 6-20 V
	C	D 14 V U 6 V	A 0-14 V B 0-14 V
RW multi-control	A	D 19 V C 9 V	U 9-19 V
	B	D 16 V C 6 V	U 6-16 V
	D	A 19 V B 16 V C 10 V	None
	U	None	A 9-19 V B 6-16 V
V (V220) Z (Z220)	U	None	A 6-25 V B 6-25 V C 6-25 V D 6-25 V
VW ZW multi-control	U	None	A* 6-20 V B 6-20 V C 6-20 V D* 6-20 V
1032 1032M 1033 1233 multi-control	A	C 16 V B 5 V	U 5-16 V
	B	C 11 V	U 0-11 V
	C	A 16 V B 11 V	None
	U	None	A 5-16 V B 0-11 V
1034	A	C 20 V B 6 V	U 10-20 V
	B	C 14 V A 6 V	U 4-14 V
	C	A 20 V B 14 V	None
	U	None	A 10-20 V B 4-14 V

*With internal whistle control

8 Bus wires

Soldering connections provides optimum performance in bus wiring.

Think of bus wires as convenient extensions of the binding post terminals on your transformer. They extend the reach of those terminals so you can avoid having a confusing jumble of wires at the control panel.

Unless your layout is very small and uncomplicated, bus wires are almost a necessity. They can be installed around the periphery of the layout or cut across it diagonally. The recommended wire size is 12 gauge or heavier, depending on the dimensions of the spread. Layouts can have as many as four or five different buses – one for the ground return, another for track feeders, and two or three different fixed voltages for lights and accessories. Unfortunately, not all Lionel accessories were designed to operate at the same voltage, so buses carrying 12, 16, and 20 volts are common.

If you install them with great care, permanent bus wires may be left bare to make hookups easy at almost any spot along the line. Obviously, the bare wires should not come in contact with other bare wires, and they should be rigidly fixed to something that doesn't conduct electricity. Wooden benchwork fills the bill nicely. Holding bare bus wires with staples, driven in every two feet or so, will keep them in place.

Yes, you should solder these bus wire connections for optimum performance. Specially tinned solid copper wire is available to make the job easier, but regular wire will do.

Without bus wiring

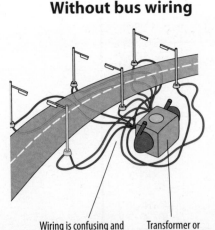

Wiring is confusing and difficult to troubleshoot

Transformer or control panel

With bus wiring

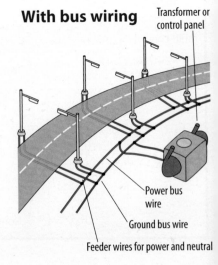

Transformer or control panel

Power bus wire

Ground bus wire

Feeder wires for power and neutral

Admittedly, many otherwise brave people cringe at the thought of soldering things together. The process is not difficult, once you learn how (see chapter 10).

If you can't overcome the solderphobia, you can try some of these alternative, albeit less satisfactory, methods of connecting accessory wires to the bus lines: Strip about an inch of insulation from the end of the accessory wire. Next, wind it tightly around the bus wire three or four times. Then, position a staple over this connection and hammer it into the wooden benchwork as hard as you can. That should keep it in place.

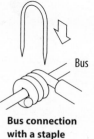

Bus connection with a staple

You can also strip about half an inch of insulation from the end of the accessory wire and loop it around the shaft of a short wood or sheet-metal screw that has a large round head. Drive the screw into the benchwork next to the bus wire. Sometimes, putting a washer on the screw helps when making this kind of connection.

There is an almost dizzying array of solderless lugs and terminals, as well as crimping tools to apply them, available at many hardware and electrical supply stores. You may find some of these items useful in wiring your layout, but they represent a long and expensive way of trying to get around learning how to solder two wires together.

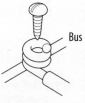

Bus connection with a screw

A star wiring system, as an alternative to bus wires, routes power via heavy wires to distribution points, or hubs, at various locations on the layout. From these hubs, feeders of lighter wire are strung, usually to power lights and accessories. The resulting wiring resembles groups of stars, hence the name.

Layout using bus wiring

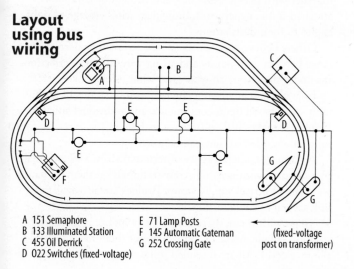

A 151 Semaphore
B 133 Illuminated Station
C 455 Oil Derrick
D 022 Switches (fixed-voltage)
E 71 Lamp Posts
F 145 Automatic Gateman
G 252 Crossing Gate

(fixed-voltage post on transformer)

9 Connections

Connectors of all types keep wiring neat and organized.

Stringing wires and making connections to track and accessories usually turns out to be somewhat of a personal matter.

Sometimes, wiring plans are carefully determined and laid out in advance, with the wires bundled into neat cables, tied together with plastic cable ties, and/or held by cup hooks attached to the benchwork. Individual wires emerge at right angles to their destinations.

Others believe that wiring should follow the shortest distance between two points and string wires in every direction. It's under the layout, so who cares what it looks like?

In practice, many layouts include combinations of both, with styles based upon convenience and individual situations. Frankly, it makes little difference, as long as the wires are carefully color-coded so they can be traced.

An almost endless variety of terminal strips and terminal blocks exists, with isolated screw terminals on them, in hardware and electrical supply stores. Bridges are also available to link several of these terminals.

To go with them, there are various types of solderless connectors – spade, hook, or loop. Some of them have insulated plastic sleeves. All are intended to be crimped to the stripped end of a wire, and special stripping and crimping tools are also available.

To join the ends of two or more wires, there are twist-on wire connectors – commonly known as wire nuts – available in sizes to match the different wire gauges.

By using only a pair of pliers, suitcase connectors (tap-splice connectors) can be used to connect feeder wires to bus wires. These connectors are color-coded: Red are for 18-22 gauge wire, and blue go with 14-18 gauge wire.

While all of these labor-savers work well and can come in handy at some point in the wiring process, they tend to be expensive when used in quantity. They are all intended to eliminate the need for soldering, which can be a problem for some people.

Face it, everyone who builds a layout will have to do some soldering on it when connecting wires, if only to attach feeder wires to the track. Those little Lockons and clips that Lionel packed with its starter sets are not capable of doing the job on a large spread. Try inserting some 18-gauge wire into one, and you will see what I mean. They just are not heavy-duty enough.

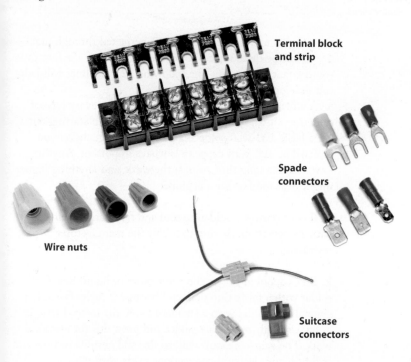

Terminal block and strip

Spade connectors

Wire nuts

Suitcase connectors

10 Successful soldering

Successful soldering can be achieved in 12 simple steps.

Soldering is an acquired skill that is perfected through practice. Don't be discouraged if you aren't good at it the first time you try. Few people are. The following 12 guidelines will help you develop the proper techniques.

A wide range of equipment is available for every type of soldering job and every experience level. When starting out, use a basic 100-watt soldering gun or iron, whichever you prefer. The 100-watt capacity is what's important. Anything lower takes a long time to heat the work, and anything higher might heat too fast for a beginner.

1. Buy or borrow a soldering tool and familiarize yourself with its operation. Be sure to follow the manufacturer's instructions.

2. Buy a spool of solder and some paste or liquid flux. Get solder with a fairly thin diameter because it melts faster. For general use, solder with a standard 60:40 tin-to-lead ratio is good. Use only rosin-core solder and rosin flux for electrical work. The acid-core stuff will oxidize and corrode in time and will ruin any electrical connections made with it.

3. Tin your new tool according to the manufacturer's directions. If your gun or iron isn't new, tin it anyway. If it is rough or pitted from use, smooth the tip first with a fine file. Then smear some flux on the tip. Turn on the tool and heat it up. Next, run a bit of solder over the tip. The solder should adhere and look shiny. If it drips down, you used too much.

A soldering iron can be used as well as a gun.

4. Practice using the gun or iron. Solder scrap wires and metal pieces together until you get the hang of the process – then practice some more.

5. Clean the surfaces of whatever you intend to solder. They must be free of rust, corrosion, oxidation, dirt, and grease. Use fine emery paper for this – even on new materials.

6. Smear flux on the areas where you want the solder to flow and adhere.

7. If possible, make a good mechanical connection first. Twist wires together as tightly as you can. Don't rely on the solder to make the connection by itself.

8. Heat the work with your soldering tool. Apply the solder to the work, not the tool.

9. Touch the heated work with the solder. Let the solder flow until you think there is enough to hold the connection firmly.

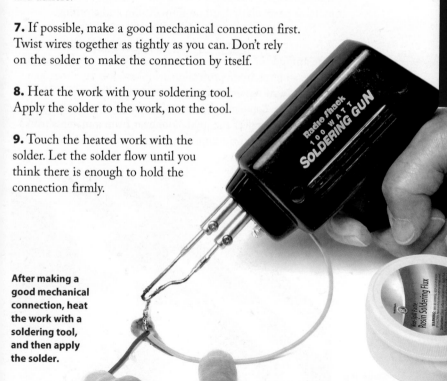

After making a good mechanical connection, heat the work with a soldering tool, and then apply the solder.

Protect soldered connections with electrician's tape or heat-shrink tubing.

10. Lift the soldering tool away from the work, but don't disturb the work itself until you are sure the solder has hardened. You usually can see it change from a liquid to a solid state in a few seconds.

11. If you don't get everything right the first time, reheat the connection. In its liquid state, solder is smooth and shiny. As it hardens, the shiny luster tones down a bit, but the overall appearance remains smooth and bright. If your finished work is dull, wrinkled, or grainy, you have a cold solder joint, which will give you trouble in the future. So reheat the work until the solder flows again, add a bit more solder if necessary, and wait for it to harden. Repeat this until you are satisfied with the result.

12. Be very careful as you solder. Do not touch the iron and watch out for excess solder dripping from the work. Molten metal is particularly hard on human skin and clothing.

To protect your newly soldered connection, you can cover it in several ways. One way is to wind good old electrician's tape around the wires like a bandage. But heat-shrink tubing makes a better, more professional-looking job. It comes in a number of different diameters and can be slipped over the wires before connecting them. When you've finished, simply slip the tubing over the joint. The heat from a match shrinks the tubing around the connection, giving it a continuous and tight-fitting covering.

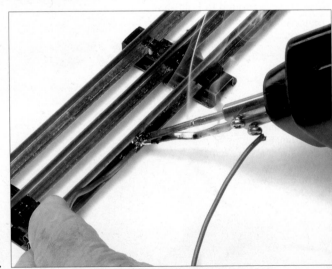

Soldering wires to track provides the best electrical connection.

Zones of control **11**

In this age of digital electronics, with several highly publicized systems of command control available for model railroad layouts, an in-depth treatment of the various types of traditional layout wiring might seem strangely out of place.

While these new systems seem to work well, they are not for everyone. They tend to be high-tech and designed for use by the very computer literate. As such, they can be a source of confusion and frustration in the hands of hobbyists who just want to run their trains. They are also expensive.

Happily, the old tried and true systems that use transformer technology are still around and serviceable at more reasonable prices. Both block and cab control can actually be more fun because they are hands-on systems, meaning operators have to be attentive at all times.

The basic concepts involved are easy to grasp, even for those of us who aren't rocket scientists or computer hackers:

- If power is going to the track, the train will run.
- The train's speed is determined by the amount of power going to the track.
- When power to the track is shut off, the train will stop.

That's all there is to understand. If you plan to run more than one train, the layout must be divided into blocks, or zones of control.

Operating Two Trains

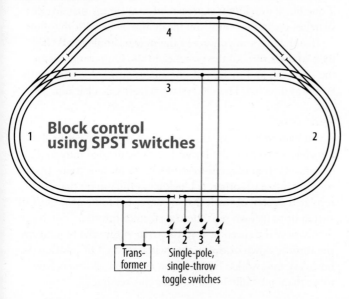

Block control using SPST switches

4

3

1

2

1 2 3 4

Trans-
former

Single-pole,
single-throw
toggle switches

Wiring a track block

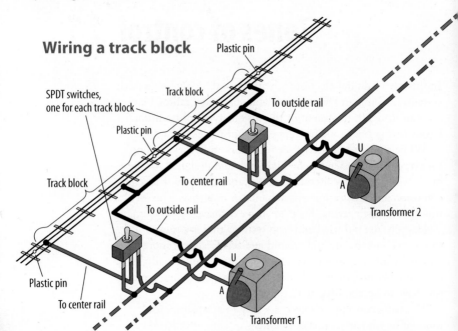

Plastic pin

SPDT switches, one for each track block

Track block

To outside rail

Plastic pin

To center rail

Track block

To outside rail

U

A

Transformer 2

Plastic pin

To center rail

U

A

Transformer 1

If you eventually plan to go with one of the new electronic control systems, you'll find that dividing your layout into blocks makes good sense anyway. With each block having its own feeder wire, the voltage drop caused by rail resistance in larger spreads will be minimized.

Blocking also makes troubleshooting easier. For example, if one block develops a short circuit, you simply turn toggle switches on and off until you locate the block with the short.

If and when you convert to the new technology, all you have to do is turn all the switches to the On position or to the same cab and then hook the electronic components to the layout as directed. The old system remains as a backup.

Block control

If you plan to run more than one train with conventional transformer control, the layout has to be divided into zones of control, often referred to as blocks, to prevent trains from running into each other. A block is nothing more than an insulated stretch of track that is connected to its own On/Off switch or to its own separate transformer throttle. To independently slow the speed or stop the train within the block, turn the throttle down or throw the switch to the Off position. See how easy that works? Some of the larger transformers have more than one built-in throttle for this reason.

To make an insulated block, pull the steel center-rail track pins from both ends of the run of track sections you want to insulate and insert plastic or fiber pins instead (available from your hobby dealer). The two outside running rails retain their metal pins. That's all there is to it.

How long should these blocks be? That depends on the size of the layout, the density of traffic, the average train length, and the location of yards, sidings, and stations. Blocks do not need to all be the same length, but they should be at least as long as your shortest mainline siding.

How many blocks are necessary? Again, there are only rules of thumb. Ideally, there should be at least three mainline blocks for two-train operation – more are probably better. Have at least one unoccupied block at all times; it can serve as a buffer zone between moving trains.

Generally speaking, turnouts are good locations to begin and end blocks because they usually indicate the boundaries between the main line and alternate routes, yards, and sidings. Also, you can easily spot the location of track turnouts from the control panel, even in the heat of operation.

At least one track of each passing siding should be a separate block to allow one train to wait while another passes. In fact, you may decide to make both such tracks insulated blocks, particularly if the siding is a long one. Yards and

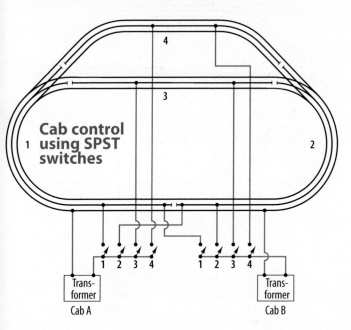

Cab control using SPST switches

industrial complexes that are large enough to permit switching operations without interfering with the main line should also be separate blocks. Finally, in most cases, you will need to insulate individual spurs. For example, each track of a locomotive storage facility ought to have its own switch to prevent waiting engines from moving until they are needed.

Block control involves only one transformer control center. The track layout is divided into insulated blocks, each having its own On/Off (single-pole, single-throw) switch or speed-controlling rheostat. Operators keep trains from running into each other by manipulating the current in the appropriate blocks by turning it off or reducing it to avoid mishaps.

Cab control systems

With cab control, there are two or more transformer control centers, or cabs, which can be operated by two or more people. The layout is divided into the same type of insulated blocks, but each block is connected to all the cabs through separate single-pole, single-throw switches in each cab. The cabs are electrically identical and autonomous, each capable of running the entire layout. As a result, the engineer in the cab is able to take his individually assigned train over the whole layout simply by energizing the appropriate blocks with his switches.

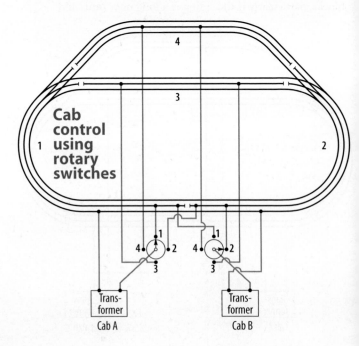

Cab control using rotary switches

According to usual cab control operating procedure, an engineer may energize only two blocks at a time – the block occupied by the train and the block ahead of it. The block the train has passed through must be shut off when the one ahead is turned on because that same block could conceivably be fed by two cabs at once, which would have strange, sometimes even disastrous, consequences.

Two variations on cab control switching deserve mention here. The first involves the use of rotary switches instead of toggles in each cab. This system requires sharp eyes and fast reflexes on the part of the engineer, who must rotate the switch knob to the next position at the exact moment the train is moving from one block to the next.

The second variation is feasible when there are only two cabs and both are in close proximity to each other. Instead of using single-pole, single-throw On/Off switches in both cabs, an operator installs one set of single-pole, double-throw switches, with Off positions in the center for common use by both cabs. Then the engineer can select the block he wants to energize by throwing the appropriate switch in his direction.

The same procedures apply with regard to using only two blocks at a time and turning off the rest, even though both cabs couldn't possibly feed the same block simultaneously.

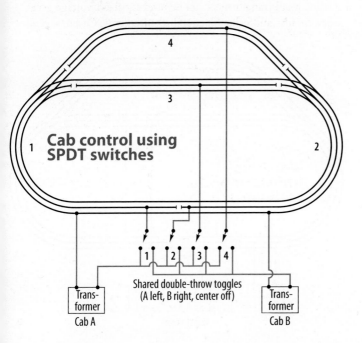

Cab control using SPDT switches

Shared double-throw toggles
(A left, B right, center off)

Trans-former
Cab A

Trans-former
Cab B

There is often some fumbling and confusion at the shared portion of the control panel as both engineers try to manipulate the same row of toggle switches. It helps if one of them is right-handed and the other is left-handed.

Individual transformers for each block

One of the most creative control systems is the embodiment of simplicity and economy. It's a variation on conventional block control that uses a battery of small transformers, one for each block, instead of one large transformer and a series of toggle switches.

With it, each block has its own individual speed control, whistle control, and reversing button, so one train can be slowed down realistically to prevent an accident with another rather than going through the equivalent of an emergency stop whenever a switch is thrown.

Onboard train whistles and horns can be activated individually, instead of having them all blow at once, with the resulting slow down of every train on the layout. Because each block has its own reversing control, the E-unit sequence reverse mechanisms need not be locked into the Forward Only position as they usually are with conventional block and cab control.

Each transformer powers one block of track, nothing more. Other small transformers can be used for fixed-voltage accessory circuits and other electrical requirements. Often, several

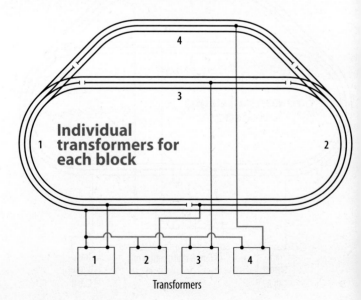

Individual transformers for each block

Transformers

fixed-voltage values are needed for different accessories. Set them up on their own transformer circuits and forget them.

Besides the versatility this system offers, the dollar savings can be substantial. Small transformers, those rated at 100 watts and under, aren't highly prized by operators or dealers, so they can often be picked up at very reasonable prices. And the supply is immense: Lionel made them by the millions, and most of them still work. Model 1063 and the earlier metal-cased 1042 transformers fit well in this application. Both are rated at 75 watts, feature whistle controls, and can handle 3 to 4 amps – enough to handle one average train on one block of track.

These small transformers don't have to be of the same type or vintage to work, although there is a certain visual appeal to a lineup of similar units. Their wattage ratings should be close to each other, so there won't be a big difference in energy level as the train moves from block to block.

Preserving the sequence-reverse function

The usual procedure when operating trains on block or cab-controlled layouts is to lock out the E-unit sequence reversing mechanisms and run all the locomotives in the Forward Only mode. That works well, but it limits operating potential.

The scheme that Lionel recommended to preserve the reversing feature of the locomotives, even though insulated blocks are used, is to jump the insulating pin going into each block with a 10-ohm, 25-watt adjustable resistor.

Another and perhaps preferable way to put such a resistor into the circuit would be across the toggle switch terminals.

With either installation, you can then adjust the resistor to permit just enough current to leak into the insulated block to keep the reverse unit's solenoid energized, although not enough to operate the locomotive's motor.

Making this adjustment on the resistor can be tricky, but it is worth the effort. Adjustable resistors of this kind can be obtained from industrial electrical or electronics supply companies.

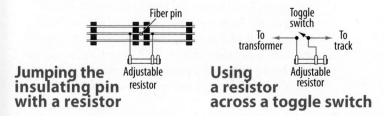

Jumping the insulating pin with a resistor

Fiber pin

Adjustable resistor

Using a resistor across a toggle switch

Toggle switch

To transformer — To track

Adjustable resistor

12 Collision prevention

A train control system prevents collisions while operating two trains.

It was the dream of every boy who grew up during the Golden Age of Toy Trains to be able to automatically run two trains on the same track without danger of a collision. Unfortunately, all we had to accomplish such a feat back then was the notoriously unreliable no. 153C contactor, which was activated by the weight of a passing train and was in constant need of adjustment. After a few bad rear-enders, most of us just gave up on the idea.

What we needed, in addition to the center-rail insulated stop section that we already had with the no. 153C contactor, was a positive device to shut off the power to the stop section when the second train was getting too close to the first one. We needed a relay!

The two systems described here use relays, positively activated by insulated running rails that can't get out of adjustment. They both operate on the same principle, but the second system is a bit more elaborate.

System One

The key is a normally closed single-pole, single-throw (SPST) relay that controls the distribution of power to the stop section, with its center rail insulated from the remainder of the layout. The stop section doesn't have to be very long. Unless you are a chronic high-baller, you need only about a three-foot section to stop a locomotive and prevent it from coasting through the dead block.

The trip section, set off by two insulated track pins in an insulated stretch of outer rail, is usually only a few track sections ahead of the stop section. It should be long enough to prevent a stopped train from starting up before there is a safe distance between the trains. While the trip section's length will depend to some degree on the size of the layout, a minimum of four to five feet is recommended.

System One

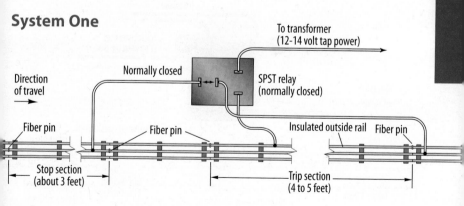

To transformer (12-14 volt tap power)

Normally closed

SPST relay (normally closed)

Direction of travel

Fiber pin

Fiber pin

Insulated outside rail   Fiber pin

Stop section (about 3 feet)

Trip section (4 to 5 feet)

System Two

This system, which is preferred by many operators, is nearly identical to System One, except that a different relay allows for multiple train control and the realistic use of track signals.

A double-pole, double-throw (DPDT) relay not only turns the track power in the stop section on and off but simultaneously allows an electrical path to switch from one light bulb to another. So you can make a red signal change to green at the same time a train powers up and leaves the stop section.

Among the two-bulb accessories that can use this system are block signals (Lionel postwar nos. 153, 163, and 353), signal bridges (no. 450), gantry signals (no. 452), and dwarf signals (no. 148).

If you have a large layout, what's great about using these systems is that you can install as many blocks as you need to prevent rear-end collisions. Keep in mind that with this system you have the added benefit of an impressive light show in each block area.

Of course, with both of these systems, locomotive reverse units are locked into the Forward Only mode. For those who want to preserve the reversing function, there is a way around this with adjustable resistors in each block.

System Two

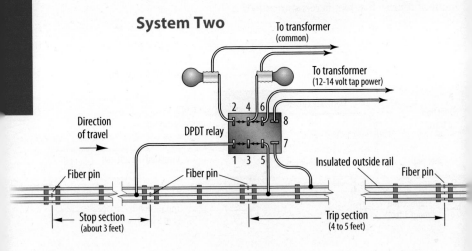

50

AC and DC relays

Relays are common in toy train control, but over the years, a shift occurred from alternating current relays to today's direct current relays.

Relay

The two systems described are designed for use with relays having a 12-volt AC coil, once a staple for automatic block control. If you have 12-volt AC relays, or know where to find some, by all means use them, as they have become scarce.

DC relays are plentiful and may be substituted with good results. However, to accommodate the DC coils, the AC current from the transformer must first be converted to DC. The simplest way to do this is with a full-wave bridge rectifier (available at many electronics stores).

The rectifier should have a voltage rating at, or above, the 12 volts needed for the coil and enough amperage capacity in the contacts to handle a multi-train layout. A minimum of 5 amps is recommended.

Rectifier

Full-wave bridge rectifiers have four terminals – pins, wires, or solder lugs – on them. The two AC input terminals are either labeled AC or designated with a sine wave (~). Connect these terminals to the transformer, or in this case, to the transformer and the insulated track section.

The two DC outputs are labeled + and -. In this application, the plus and minus designations make no difference. Just wire one of them to one end of the relay coil and wire the other one to the other end. That's it.

The wiring diagram below shows how these rectifiers should be wired into the circuit ahead of the DC relay coil.

Converting AC current from a transformer to DC

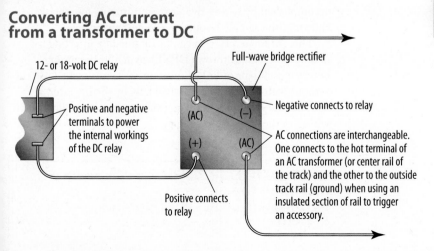

12- or 18-volt DC relay

Full-wave bridge rectifier

Positive and negative terminals to power the internal workings of the DC relay

(AC)

(–)

Negative connects to relay

(+)

(AC)

AC connections are interchangeable. One connects to the hot terminal of an AC transformer (or center rail of the track) and the other to the outside track rail (ground) when using an insulated section of rail to trigger an accessory.

Positive connects to relay

13 Automatic route selection

Wiring two or more turnouts together can allow a train to select its route automatically.

The automatic non-derailing feature, which Lionel pioneered and incorporated into all of its turnouts (and adopted by other manufacturers), worked on the principle of the insulated running rail. A short section of rail on both routes was insulated so that, if the turnout was thrown against an approaching train, the wheels and axles of that train would bridge the rails, complete the electrical circuit, and, in the last second, throw the turnout in the right direction, so the train would not derail.

The non-derailing feature can be used in a system in which the train itself automatically selects different routes. This is accomplished by wiring two or more turnouts together as shown in the sample layouts on the next two pages.

This automated system can be disabled by inserting a double-pole, single-throw (DPST) switch in the wiring between each pair of linked turnouts. When switched off, the turnouts can be controlled individually by the operator. It is not necessary to unhook the normal turnout controllers when wiring in the automated system.

DPST switch disabling the automated system

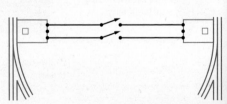

Sample layouts

The following four simple layouts use automatic train control and illustrate the principles involved, which you can apply to your own layout.

Basic two-oval layout

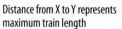

Distance from X to Y represents maximum train length

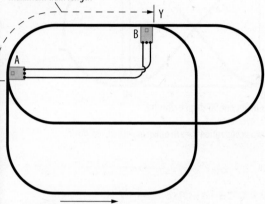

One pair of turnouts, one 90-degree crossing
Two passes to cover layout
Turnouts thrown in unison: green-green, red-red

Interconnected two-oval layout

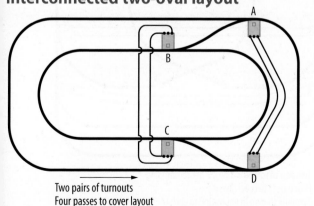

Two pairs of turnouts
Four passes to cover layout
Turnouts thrown in opposition to each other: green-red, red-green

Double cross layout

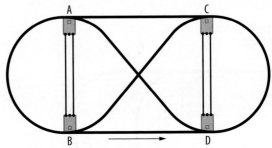

Two pair of turnouts, one 90-degree crossing
Four passes to cover layout
Turnouts thrown in opposition to each other: green-red, red-green

Christmas tree layout

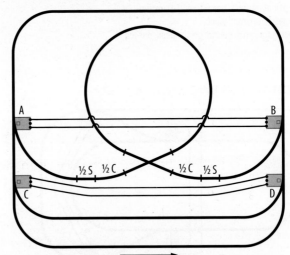

Two pair of turnouts, one 45-degree crossing
Four passes to cover layout
Turnouts thrown in opposition to each other: green-red, red-green
Some half straight and half curve sections required

Train-activated accessories 14

Lionel accessories were operated with four different contactors.

Using Accessories and Controllers

For decades, Lionel train-activated accessories were sold with special contactors that made them operate. There were four different ones.

145C and 153C were adjustable, spring-loaded switches that fit under the track and responded to the weight of the passing train. The others, 154C and 1045C, had insulated contact plates that snapped into place over one of the two running rails. The metal wheels and axles of the passing train momentarily completed an electrical circuit between the other running rail and the insulated plate.

All four worked well enough to keep a kid who ran his trains around the Christmas tree or on the rec room floor happy. However, for permanent model railroad layouts, they fell somewhat short. The spring-loaded contactors were notorious for working themselves out of adjustment regularly, while the contact-plate models needed help in the realism department.

Gateman connected with 153C contactor

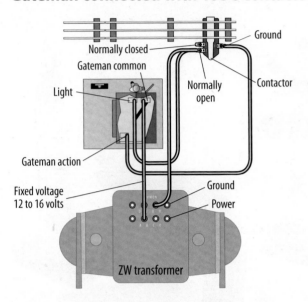

Ground
Normally closed
Gateman common
Light
Normally open
Contactor
Gateman action
Fixed voltage 12 to 16 volts
Ground
Power
ZW transformer

Gateman connected with insulated track section

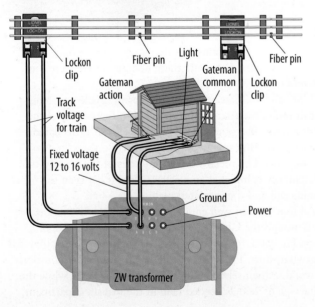

Lockon clip
Fiber pin
Light
Gateman action
Gateman common
Lockon clip
Fiber pin
Track voltage for train
Fixed voltage 12 to 16 volts
Ground
Power
ZW transformer

145C contactor

This was the most common spring-loaded Lionel contactor. It functioned as a simple single-pole, single-throw switch. The weight of the train overhead forced the contacts together and completed the electrical circuit to the accessory. The no. 145C came with the following accessories:

> 45 and 145 Gateman
> 140 Banjo Signal
> 151 Semaphore
> 155 Ringing Signal
> 252 Crossing Gate
> 262 Highway Crossing Signal

153C contactor

Intended to operate two-light (red and green) block signals, the no. 153C was a single-pole double-throw switch, with the normally closed position connected to the green light. With the weight of the passing train, the green light connection would be opened, and the connection with the red light temporarily closed. When the train passed, the contactor spring would return it to normal, and the signal would again show green.

The 153C came with the 153, 163, and 353 two-light block signals. Many operators also used it to automate the no. 148 Dwarf Signal.

By using a center-rail insulated block at the signal, and connecting its power to the green light terminal on the contactor, a basic form of automatic two-train control could be achieved.

154C contactor

This specialized insulated-plate contactor was packed only with the no. 154 Highway Flashing Signal. The plate was divided into two sections, corresponding to the two lights on the signal. Contact made by the wheels of the passing train would cause the lights to blink intermittently in a charming, albeit not particularly realistic, way.

1045C contactor

This also was a one-accessory contactor. It came with the no. 1045 Flagman. Contact made by the train wheels would make the flagman raise his warning flag. It would drop in a staccato motion after each wheel set passed.

Crossing gate connected with 153C contactor

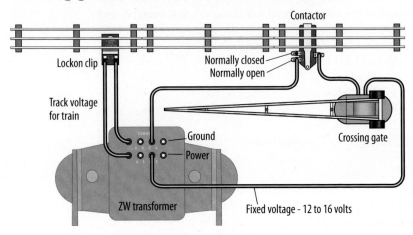

Contactor

Lockon clip

Normally closed
Normally open

Track voltage
for train

Ground

Power

Crossing gate

ZW transformer

Fixed voltage - 12 to 16 volts

Crossing gate connected with insulated track section

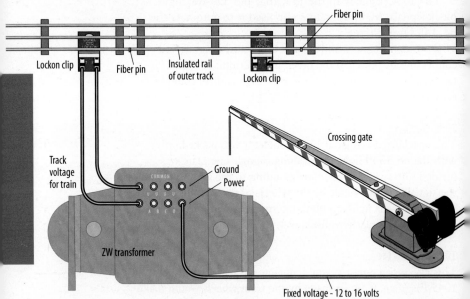

Fiber pin

Lockon clip

Fiber pin

Insulated rail
of outer track

Lockon clip

Track
voltage
for train

Ground
Power

Crossing gate

ZW transformer

Fixed voltage - 12 to 16 volts

Insulated running rails

A far better way to activate accessories is by connecting them to an insulated running rail and allowing the metal train wheels and axles complete the electrical circuit. This method does everything the 145C, 154C, and 1045C can do and probably even more. Here are some additional advantages:

- Insulated rails never go out of adjustment. Of course, they have to be kept reasonably clean.

- There is positive action throughout the length of the train. They work just as well from the loco to the caboose in spite of weight discrepancies.

- Any number of insulated track sections can be used in a run to provide longer approaches to crossing gates, signals, and the like.

- Loose track sections do not bob up and down. They can be securely fastened and even ballasted.

- While unsightly contactor mechanisms stick out, accessory wires can be discretely soldered in place.

To wire an accessory to be activated by an insulated running rail, attach one wire to the insulated rail and the other to the center rail or a fixed-voltage power source.

You can buy insulated running rail sections or make your own. Lionel and others offer ready-made straight sections, but you can save money by making them yourself. It's easy to do and you can put insulated sections anywhere, even on curves.

Begin by bending the tie clips upward and removing one of the running rails from the section to be insulated. Then take the fiber center-rail insulators from a discarded track section and slip them on the loose rail. (Cardboard or electrical tape may be used instead.) Crimp it back in place. Put plastic or fiber insulating pins into both ends of the rail to isolate it electrically from the rest of the track. That's all there is to it.

If you make your own, you can get creative. For instance, instead of using 154C and 1045C contactors to operate the highway flasher and the flagman, which require short, intermittent contacts, you can insulate short pieces of rail within a normal section and wire appropriately. More ties should be added to this track to strengthen the reconstruction.

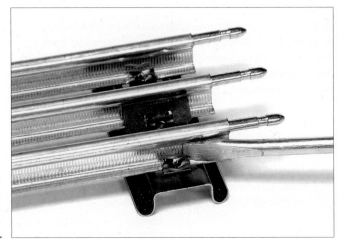

To insulate a running rail, use a screwdriver to bend the tie clip and remove the running rail.

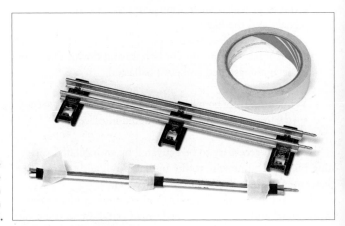

Masking tape can keep the insulation in place when replacing the rail.

Replace the rail, crimp it in place, and put an insulating pin into both ends.

Insulating short pieces of rail

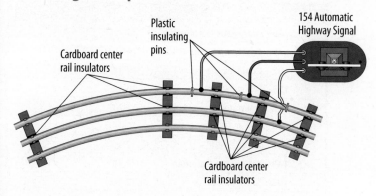

Plastic insulating pins

154 Automatic Highway Signal

Cardboard center rail insulators

Cardboard center rail insulators

That takes care of replacing the 145C, 154C, and 1045C contactors. Replacing the 153C contactor requires the use of a relay in addition to the insulated rail.

Accessory operating voltages

The list of operating voltages for Lionel postwar accessories on page 62 contains voltages that were specified in official service literature. For the rest, we can only guess or, better yet, experiment with to find a happy (or at least a working) medium of some kind.

Lionel uses the word *variable* when describing these input voltages for some accessories. For the 350 Transfer Table and 375 Turntable, the voltage level (the speed of operation) is probably a matter of personal operator preference. The 356 Freight Station, 362 Barrel Loader, 464 Lumber Mill, and 494 Rotary Beacon are powered by notoriously hard-to-adjust vibration motors. Probably because each motor has characteristics that make it unique, the optimum input voltage can't be generalized and must be determined by experimenting.

Some operators connect small, individual starter-set transformers to each vibration-motor accessory, so they can adjust the throttles to provide the optimum individual voltage level.

It is easy to see why some larger, accessory-laden layouts often have as many as three different fixed-voltage accessory buses. The three voltage ranges commonly used are 10-12, 14-16, and 18-20. The first two accommodate most of the listed accessories, while the third is reserved for turnout motors.

Operating voltages for Lionel postwar accessories

Number	Accessory	Input voltage
45	Automatic Gateman	12
75	Tear Drop Lamp	14
97	Coal Elevator	12-16
125	Whistling Station	10-14
128	Animated Newsstand	11-13
138	Water Tower	10-14
140	Banjo Signal	12-16
145	Automatic Gateman	12-14
153	Block Signal	12-14
161	Mail Bag Pickup	10-14
164	Lumber Loader	12-16
165	Magnet Crane	10-15
175	Rocket Launcher	9-12
182	Magnet Crane	12-16
193	Flashing Tower	12-16
195	Floodlight Tower	12-14
252	Crossing Gate	10-14
264	Fork Lift Platform	9-14
313	Bascule Bridge	14 (approximate)
342	Culvert Pipe Loader	9-14
345	Culvert Pipe Unloader	9-14
350	Transfer Table	Variable
356	Freight Station	Variable
362	Barrel Loader	Variable
364	Lumber Loader	12-14
375	Turntable	Variable
395	Floodlight Tower	12-14
397	Coal Loader	12-15
410	Billboard Blinker	12-16
415	Fueling Station	12-16
450	Signal Bridge	12-16
455	Oil Derrick	12-14
456	Coal Ramp	12-14
464	Lumber Mill	Variable
494	Rotary Beacon	Variable

Ganged controllers 15

Ganging controllers, hooking up one controller to activate two or more similar remote controlled devices, is usually done for convenience or for saving valuable space on the control panel. Toy train control boxes were designed for around-the-tree or living-room-floor operations without any consideration of size.

While I have seen accessory controllers ganged in a multitude of innovative ways, and for various good reasons, the two most common and logical applications are with uncouple/unload track sections and remote control turnouts.

UCS remote control sections

Since the electromagnet (uncouple) and the control rails (unload) on a UCS remote control track section work only when there is a coupler or an operating car in place over them, it doesn't matter if several are ganged together on one controller.

This particularly makes sense in yards or other locations where several UCS remote sections are in close proximity to each other – within one frame of vision for the operator. I've seen large layouts with four or five of them wired together with excellent results.

Linking two or more UCS remote control track sections is quite simple. Connect the four wires from the controller cable to the numbered terminals (1, 2, 3, 4) on the track as usual.

Then run four more wires from each of the numbered terminals on the first section to the like-numbered terminals on the second section.

For a third section, do the same thing, using the second section as your starting point. Continue on for as many sections as you wish.

Remote control turnouts

For convenience, the throw mechanisms of two (or more) remote control turnouts may also be ganged for operation by one controller. Of course, this is practical only in situations where the turnouts always need to be thrown at the same time and in the same relationship to each other.

The most obvious examples are on crossovers between tracks or on semi-automated layouts where the position of one key turnout determines the route the train is to take.

Ganged UCS tracks

How to wire ganged UCS tracks is shown here.

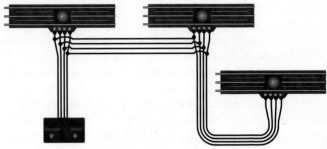

Crossover

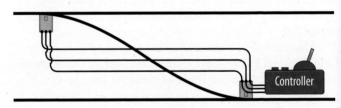

Automatic route selection with non-derailing turnouts

Controller used as an override for the system

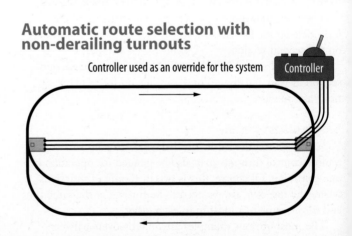

Replacement controllers 16

Original controllers for accessories were small and easily lost. Many had Bakelite cases, which often cracked or shattered upon even moderate impact. As a result, there are a lot more postwar accessories around than there are controllers.

Improvising replacements for many of them is easier than you might think. Some require only a simple toggle switch, a momentary-contact push button, or a combination of these.

Controller with broken Bakelite case

Push-button accessories

The Lionel postwar accessories listed below need only a basic push button to complete their electrical circuits and make them operate. Almost any kind of push button can be used.

No.	Accessory
30	Water Tower
114	Newsstand with horn
118	Newsstand with whistle
125	Whistling Station
138	Water Tower
161	Mail Bag Pickup
257	Freight Station with horn
313	Bascule Bridge
334	Dispatching Board
415	Fueling Station

SPST accessories

The following accessories were packed with a single-pole, single-throw (SPST) On/Off switch. Again, any kind of On/Off switch can be used.

No.	Accessory
128	Animated Newsstand
264	Fork Lift Platform
342	Culvert Pipe Loader
345	Culvert Pipe Unloader
356	Freight Station
362	Barrel Loader
364	Lumber Loader
397	Coal Loader
464	Lumber Mill

This no. 97 Coal Elevator has been wired with a replacement controller.

Other controllers

The no. 97 Coal Elevator and the no. 164 Lumber Loader had both push buttons and SPST switches on their controllers. The three lead wires from the controllers were connected to numbered terminals on the accessories. The controllers, and the way their functions were wired, are identical on both.

No. 97 Coal Loader controller

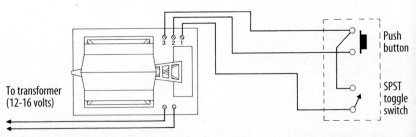

To transformer (12-16 volts)

Push button

SPST toggle switch

No. 456C Coal Ramp controller

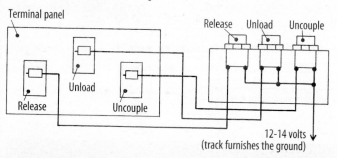

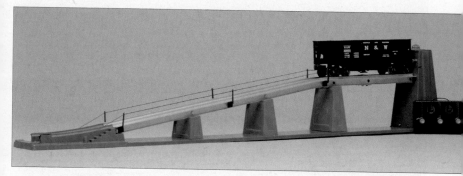

The controller for the 456C Coal Ramp was unique to the accessory. Three push buttons handled the uncouple, unload, and release functions. To fabricate one, start by mounting three SPST momentary-contact push-button switches in a row. Each switch has two terminals. Wire all three switches together, using one terminal on each. Run three wires from the remaining terminals to the three posts on the coal ramp. Connect a single wire from the three interconnected terminals to a fixed-voltage post on your transformer (12-14 volts are recommended). The track serves as the ground return.

The controller for the 456C Coal Ramp controller used push buttons to operate its uncouple, unload, and release functions.

Coal ramp replacement controller

No. 497C Coal Station controller

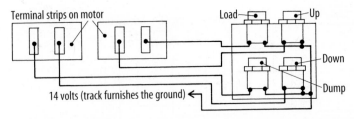

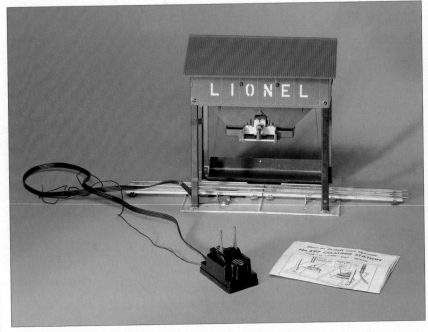

The 497C Coaling Station controller employed two levers to operate four functions.

The 497C Coaling Station came with a four-function controller that used two levers for activation. While it would be difficult to improvise such a controller, we found that substituting four SPST momentary-contact push buttons would yield the same results.

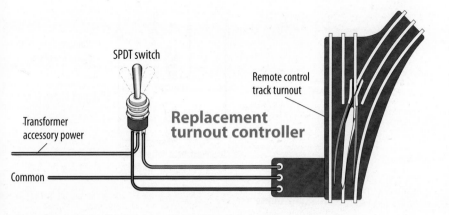

022 turnouts

The ubiquitous Lionel 022 track turnouts, and many similar O gauge products that followed the pattern over the years, came equipped with impressive lever-action controllers having red and green indicator lights on them.

If you can forego the indicator lights, a functional replacement can be fabricated with a momentary-contact, single-pole, double-throw (SPDT) toggle switch that has a center Off position. This will work just like the lever in the original controller.

If you can't find a toggle switch with all of these specifications, any SPDT with a center Off position can be substituted. But you'll have to remember to manually return the switch to the Off position immediately after the turnout is thrown. Otherwise, the non-derailing feature won't work, and the solenoid coils in the unit will eventually burn out.

Dwarf signal

The versatile controller for the 148 Dwarf Signal was nothing more than an SPDT switch that could be wired in several ways:

- To change the signal light from green to red.

- To interlock the signal with an insulated track block to stop the train when the lights change.

- To be used with other signals and insulated blocks to provide a system of multiple train control for the entire layout.

UCS wiring

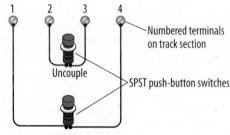

Numbered terminals on track section

Uncouple

SPST push-button switches

To unload, both buttons must be pushed simultaneously

UCS controllers

The five-rail UCS remote control track section serves as both an uncoupling and unloading location for Lionel postwar rolling stock. The uncoupling function is handled by an electromagnet in the center of the section. The unloading function for operating freight cars is controlled by two pairs of rails, right and left of the magnet.

The two-button UCS controller contains a four-layer wafer switch that looks dauntingly complicated. It isn't really, but to replace it, you need an SPST switch and a DPST momentary-contact push button. The push button might be hard to find at your local electronics store.

A quite satisfactory alternative can be made by using two SPST momentary-contact push-button switches, wired as shown above.

This alternative is a lot easier to wire, but it requires a departure from the operational norm. The uncoupling button is used by itself, but to energize the unloading function, both buttons must be pushed simultaneously.

All things considered, the best option might be to find a used UCS controller, still in working condition, at a swap meet or in a hobby shop clearance bin. They are by no means scarce commodities since Lionel made millions of them over the years.

Almost any simple toggle or push-button switches of the right configurations can be used when improvising replacement controllers for Lionel postwar accessories. While the current drain for most accessories is less than for trains, switches with at least 3- to 5-amp ratings should be used throughout.

If your layout has a control panel, your replacement controllers can be built right in. If not, they can be housed in small metal or plastic boxes. If you are good with sheet metal, you can even bend your own. Improvise – that's the name of the game.

Quick fixes 17

This chapter covers several miscellaneous situations that you might encounter when wiring your layout.

Wiring two intersecting independent routes

Lionel crossings, often referred to as crossovers, were constructed with electrical continuity maintained on both intersecting routes. They must be modified if two independently controlled routes are expected to cross over each other. It is a fairly easy job, involving removal of the sheet-metal stamping on the underside of the crossing and replacing it with two wires.

First, bend the fingers holding the sheet-metal stamping just enough so the stamping can be removed. Then, bend the fingers back into position against the insulators, so the rails are again seated firmly in place.

Solder short pieces of 18-gauge wire, basically creating electrical bridges that link the linear center rails while keeping the intersecting routes electrically isolated from each other.

Wire bridges link a crossing's center rails and keep intersecting routes isolated.

Fixed voltage for remote control track sections

Using fixed voltage on UCS or 6019 remote control track sections improves performance and allows them to function even when track power is off. The simple conversion involves only one wire.

To change a UCS track section to fixed-voltage operation, unhook the number 3 wire in the cable (counting from the left) from its terminal on the track section and connect it to a 15-volt accessory bus or directly to a similar post on the transformer.

For some reason, Lionel designed the 027 tracks differently, so with an 027 gauge 6019 remote control track, disconnect the number 4 wire instead.

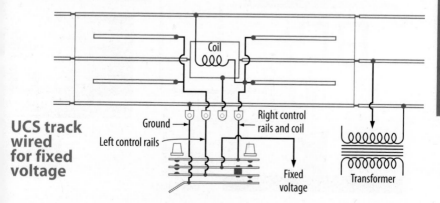

UCS track wired for fixed voltage

Coil

Ground

Left control rails

Right control rails and coil

Fixed voltage

Transformer

Warning lights for hidden trackage

No matter how well planned and designed, there always seems to be a few blind spots on every layout that could be a problem – the inside of a long tunnel, behind a scenic backdrop, or some other place where the track can't be seen from the operator's control position.

Dick Christianson had some troublesome ones on his long gone, but probably never-to-be-forgotten by those who saw it, Lionel Lines/Santa Fe layout (featured in *Build a Better Toy Train Layout*). He and John Grams solved the

Insulated track sections used for warning lights on a hidden spur

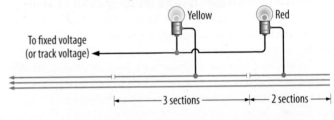

Wiring diagram for warning lights

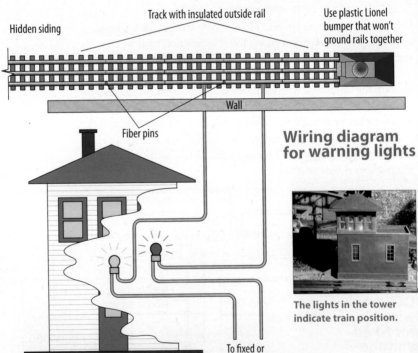

The lights in the tower indicate train position.

visibility problems with a series of colored warning lights on the control panels and elsewhere. What they did can be a guide to solving similar situations on your model railroad.

The warning lights were all connected to a fixed-voltage circuit, and in the first two cases that follow, were triggered by an insulated running rail.

The freight yard lead, which also doubled as a switchback, ran under a bridge and then disappeared behind a backdrop for about 10 feet before ending. Using two separate runs of insulated track sections and red and yellow lights, the operator can chart the progress of the hidden train.

The yellow caution light went on to indicate that the train was five track sections (about 50 inches) from the end of the line. The red light meant the train was only two sections (20 inches) away, so it was time to stop.

Dick decided to mount the two lights in the control tower at the head of the yard. In plain sight to all, this tower actually served a function on the layout.

A long, behind-the-backdrop passing siding, which was a convenient place to store a full-length train, posed an even greater problem. There was no way of seeing when a train was entering the siding or when it was leaving.

A four-light indicator on the control panel solved it: One siding was green, and the other was red. Short insulated rails at both ends of the two routes would make the control panel lights blink, indicating the train's position.

To guard against mishaps, a single-pole, double-throw switch routed the track power to one siding or to the other.

The passenger terminal's lead track disappears into a tunnel.

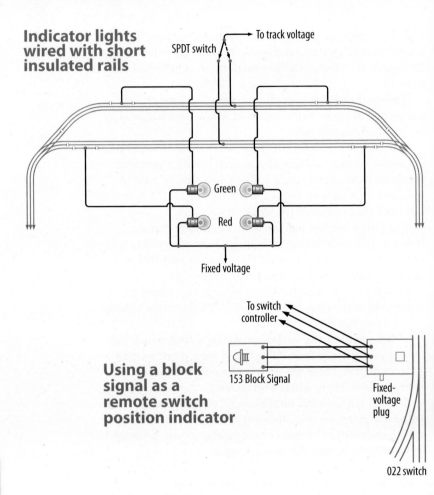

Indicator lights wired with short insulated rails

SPDT switch

To track voltage

Green

Red

Fixed voltage

Using a block signal as a remote switch position indicator

To switch controller

153 Block Signal

Fixed-voltage plug

022 switch

The lead track from the passenger terminal disappeared into a tunnel and emerged at a mainline turnout on the other side of a hill. Dick and John rigged a no. 153 Block Signal to indicate red when the turnout was set for the main line and green when it was thrown to allow a train to leave the station and enter the high iron.

They ran three wires from the signal's terminals to the three terminals on the turnout mechanism. Then, the sliding contacts that changed the controller's indication from red to green changed the signal bulbs the same way. To get a reverse indication, simply switch the two outer wires leading to the block signal.

Multimeters 18

You can probably live without a multimeter, but once you get used to having one, you'll wonder why you didn't buy it long ago. A multimeter is particularly useful if you have an operating layout with blocks, feeders, turnouts, lights, and accessories to maintain or if you do your own service and repair work on rolling stock.

Common uses for a multimeter on a layout include
• Regulating track voltage
• Setting fixed voltages for accessories and turnouts
• Finding voltage drops in trackwork and wiring
• Tracing continuity of wires and connections in circuits
• Checking the function of electrical switch contacts
• Locating short circuits in track, wiring, and accessories
• Phasing transformers

Whether you buy an analog or digital meter makes little difference. Some people want to see a numerical digital readout on a screen, while others prefer the classic look of an analog meter, with its needle sweeping across an arc of graduated scales. Both work equally well. All you really need is the most basic and inexpensive model you can find. Whichever multimeter you use, remember to read the instruction booklet carefully before using your meter and always turn your meter to the Off position when not in use.

When using an analog multimeter on lower voltages, the 15V ACV position provides more precise readings.

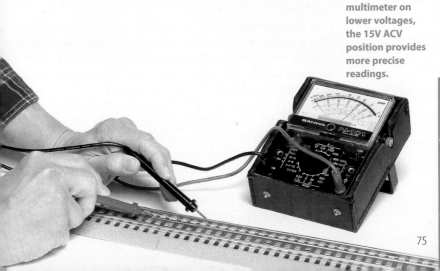

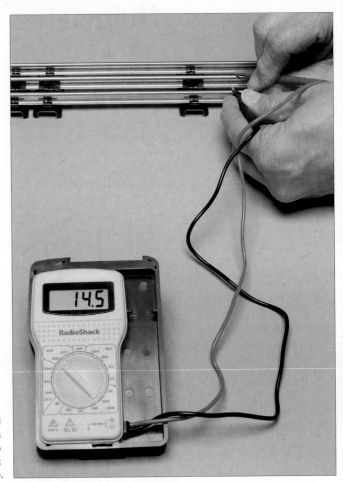

A digital multimeter is being used to measure track voltage.

Measuring voltage

Find the most appropriate AC voltage scale available for toy train use. That would be the closest upper meter range higher than the voltage you want to measure. The general range for toy trains is zero to about 25 volts (AC). If you select a lower meter range, you might damage the instrument.

Using the pictured meters as examples, the digital model should be set on the 200V ACV position. This will provide the most accurate direct numerical readout on the screen.

The analog model has a convenient 150V ACV position. To use this, you simply multiply the reading shown on the bottom 15-volt scale by 10. For a more precise reading on lower voltages, you may use the 15V ACV position but make sure the transformer output voltage is kept below that level.

Checking electrical circuit continuity

To measure circuit continuity, or lack thereof, use the meter position that indicates ohms (Ω) of resistance.

The analog meter has only one of these, 1K (1,000 ohms). The digital meter has five range choices. While they all will work, the 2,000 ohm (2K Ω) position is best because it provides a very stable reading in this application.

Full circuit continuity is indicated by a reading of zero on the ohms scale. If you experience poor or intermittent continuity, which can be caused by a bad connection or loose or dirty contacts, you will get a reading other than a steady zero.

Finding the source of a short circuit is easy with a multimeter. You'll find continuity where there should be none.

This analog multimeter is set to measure ohms of resistance.

19 Amp and volt meters

Many serious model railroaders have installed voltage and amperage meters on their control panels. While not absolutely essential to operations, they provide an added dimension of sophistication, and operators, knowing their track power is constantly being monitored, gain a sense of control.

What the meters do

A volt meter measures the amount of voltage (output) being delivered to the tracks, while an amp meter shows the amount of amperage (current) the locomotive is drawing at any given moment.

The most practical application for the volt meter is in determining approximate train speed. While there is no actual readout in scale miles per hour – voltage requirements can vary quite a bit from loco to loco – the meter will at least give you a ballpark indication. That in itself may keep you from highballing the train too fast for the curves.

The amp meter helps keep tabs on the condition of your engines. A locomotive that draws an excessive amount of amperage may be in need of repair or routine lubrication, cleaning, and maintenance.

And an amp meter will always indicate an overload or a short circuit long before the transformer's circuit breaker kicks in.

When installed on a control panel, amp and volt meters provide continuous monitoring.

A volt meter can be used to indicate approximate train speed.

An amp meter helps monitor engine condition and indicates transformer overload.

Connecting a volt meter

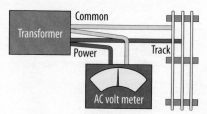

Connecting an amp meter

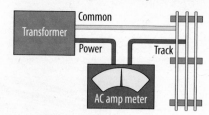

Selecting the right meters

Whether you select classic analog meters, with their needles that sweep in graceful arcs across the scales, or new digital models that present numerical readings, often down to several decimal places, makes absolutely no difference. In this application, it simply is a matter of personal preference.

It is important to buy meters that register in the proper ranges. That means zero to at least 25 or 30 volts for a volt meter, and zero to about 10 amps for an amp meter. Broader ranges tend to obscure the accuracy of the readings, particularly on analog instruments.

Also, both must be AC (alternating current) meters. Many of the meters found in electronics stores today are intended for use with DC (direct current), and they won't work with toy trains. To find the correct ones, you may have to shop around or order them from electronics suppliers.

If you are using a Lionel ZW transformer, and don't mind paying a bit more for convenience, Lionel sells a pair of digital meters that fit right on the transformer.

Installation

Ideally, a set of these meters should be installed for each transformer-powered circuit, but most operators settle for one set to monitor the track circuit only.

Hooking up voltage and amperage meters is really a simple job. As shown above, the volt meter is connected across the two transformer terminals being used for the track circuit.

The amp meter is connected in line (series) with the center-rail leg of the track circuit.

20 022 turnouts

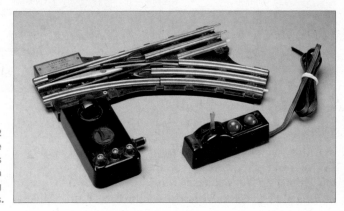

The first choice of operators for generations, Lionel's 022 turnouts were manufactured from the late 1930s to the late 1960s, revived and renumbered 5132/5133 in 1980, and made for another 14 years. Lionel's O-72 gauge turnouts share many 022 parts, including the mechanisms, so many of these tips also apply to them.

Well designed and solidly constructed from the start, these turnouts are complex electro-mechanical devices with many moving parts. Much could go wrong, but it usually doesn't as long as they are kept clean and well-maintained.

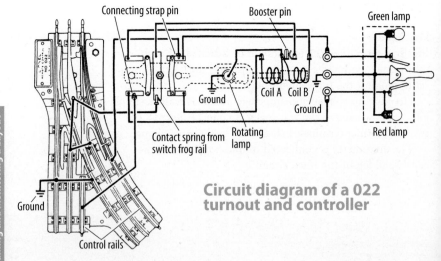

Connecting strap pin · Booster pin · Green lamp · Ground · Coil A · Coil B · Ground · Red lamp · Contact spring from switch frog rail · Rotating lamp · Ground · Control rails

Circuit diagram of a 022 turnout and controller

While repair techniques are beyond the scope of this book, here are some routine maintenance tips that will keep your 022s on your layout and out of the shop.

Clean and tune your 022 turnouts as needed, either when the action becomes erratic or sluggish or after long periods of storage. Check for both dirt and oxidation.

Use a ScotchBrite pad to remove dirt from the turnout rails and to shine the rails as well. Follow up with a little WD-40 on a soft cloth to remove the residue left by the scouring pad and shine the Bakelite base and motor case. (Never use steel wool on any track.)

Each time the motor is serviced, clean the four fixed contacts under the moving contact assembly, even if they don't appear to need it. Spray them with Control/Contact Cleaner & Lubricant (RadioShack part 64-4315) or another aerosol contact cleaner. A little solvent, such as mineral spirits, on a cotton swab will also work.

Clean out the coil and plunger by spraying contact cleaner directly into the tube. Again, mineral spirits on a cotton swab is a good alternative.

Lubricate the turnout sparingly in the following manner:

- Put one drop of oil on the lantern retainer pivot

- Apply a light film of grease where the rack slides under the lamp bracket assembly

- Lightly apply grease to the two slots of the moving contact assembly to ease friction with the retaining pins

- If needed, place a dab of grease where the front and rear of the moving contact assembly ride on the motor base

- Add a light film of grease on the sheet-metal formations over which the lock hinge rides

- Put a drop of oil on both ends of the lock hinge itself

Again, a cautionary word to use all these lubricants very sparingly. Too much of a good thing will clog up the works. The Lionel service diagram on the following page will help you identify the parts of a 022 turnout.

Control/Contact Cleaner may also be known as TV Tuner Control Cleaner.

Parts of a 022 turnout

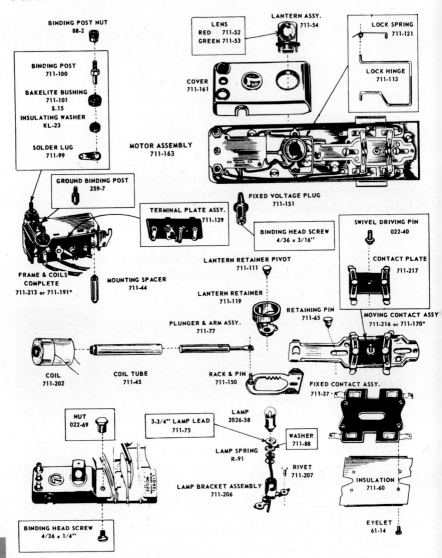

BINDING POST NUT
88-2

BINDING POST
711-100

BAKELITE BUSHING
711-101
$.15

INSULATING WASHER
KL-23

SOLDER LUG
711-99

MOTOR ASSEMBLY
711-163

GROUND BINDING POST
259-7

LENS
RED   711-52
GREEN 711-53

LANTERN ASSY.
711-54

COVER
711-161

LOCK SPRING
711-121

LOCK HINGE
711-113

FIXED VOLTAGE PLUG
711-151

TERMINAL PLATE ASSY.
711-129

BINDING HEAD SCREW
4/36 x 3/16''

SWIVEL DRIVING PIN
022-40

CONTACT PLATE
711-217

FRAME & COILS
COMPLETE
711-213 or 711-191*

MOUNTING SPACER
711-44

LANTERN RETAINER PIVOT
711-111

LANTERN RETAINER
711-119

RETAINING PIN
711-65

MOVING CONTACT ASSY
711-216 or 711-170*

PLUNGER & ARM ASSY.
711-77

COIL
711-202

COIL TUBE
711-45

RACK & PIN
711-150

FIXED CONTACT ASSY.
711-37

NUT
022-69

3-3/4'' LAMP LEAD
711-75

LAMP
2026-58

WASHER
711-88

LAMP SPRING
R-91

RIVET
711-207

LAMP BRACKET ASSEMBLY
711-206

INSULATION
711-60

BINDING HEAD SCREW
4/36 x 1/4''

EYELET
61-14

Troubleshooting 21

While every layout is somewhat different and requires its own troubleshooting methodology, a few generalizations can be made to guide the process.

Start simple but cover everything and test after each step.

Begin by taking all the locomotives and cars off the track. Examine the track carefully for foreign objects that might have fallen on it or between the rails.

Visually inspect the wiring for signs of overheating such as discolored or melted insulation.

Analyze recent events. Did you change anything? Did any visiting operators throw the wrong switch or leave you with some other unintentional surprise? Were the kids in the train room? How about the family pets? Did you notice anything that was working strangely the last time you ran your trains?

While some problems can manifest themselves intermittently or over time, look for an immediate cause.

Checking circuits

For the following troubleshooting steps, you will need a multimeter (see chapter 18). A multimeter will help you find where any circuits might be broken or shorted, but it can also indicate deviations in voltage.

Check the transformer itself. Is the output voltage as measured consistent with specifications?

Disconnect one circuit at a time and test after each change.

If you have a block system on your track, throw one switch at a time.

Check each circuit completely before going to the next one.

Be methodical and thorough. If you check every circuit, every wire, and every connection, you will eventually find the problem.

Layout wiring examples

Here are nine sample layouts that provide examples of common wiring arrangements that you may employ on your model railroad. They are followed by a section detailing how to wire an automatic two-trolley line.

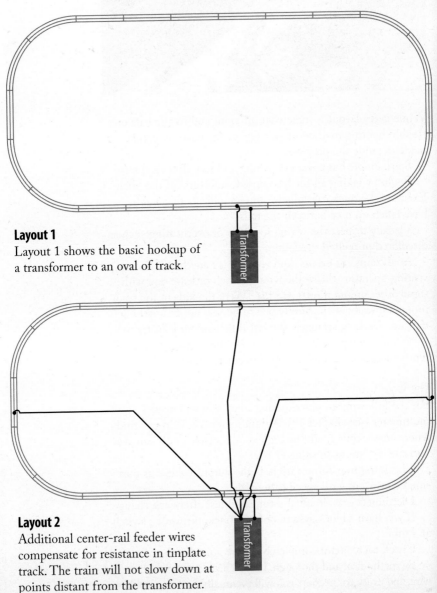

Layout 1
Layout 1 shows the basic hookup of a transformer to an oval of track.

Layout 2
Additional center-rail feeder wires compensate for resistance in tinplate track. The train will not slow down at points distant from the transformer.

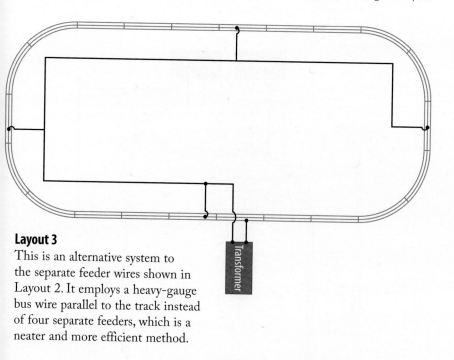

Layout 3

This is an alternative system to the separate feeder wires shown in Layout 2. It employs a heavy-gauge bus wire parallel to the track instead of four separate feeders, which is a neater and more efficient method.

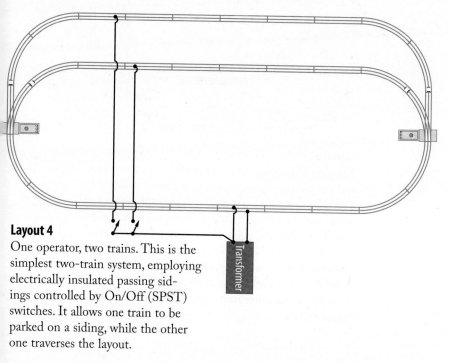

Layout 4

One operator, two trains. This is the simplest two-train system, employing electrically insulated passing sidings controlled by On/Off (SPST) switches. It allows one train to be parked on a siding, while the other one traverses the layout.

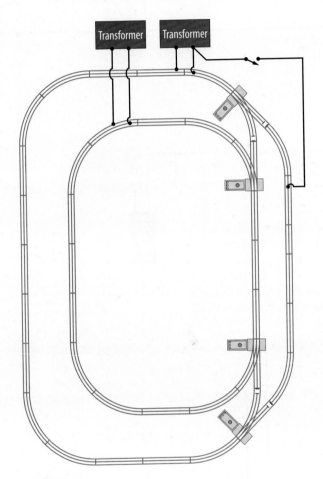

Layout 5

This layout features one or two operators, two trains, and two separate power sources or throttles. Train A, which has been running on the outer route, is parked in the switched passing siding. Then, from the inner oval, Train B ventures onto the outer track. When Train B is on the far side of the outer route, Train A starts up. Train B is then parked in the siding, while Train A is switched to the inner track. Then, Train B starts up on the outer route, while Train A runs on the inner one.

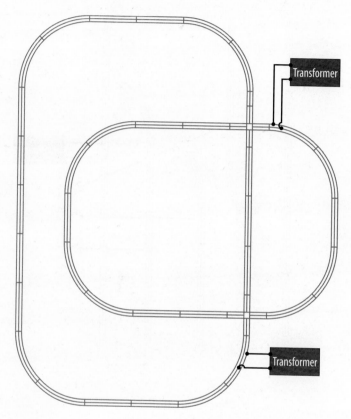

Layout 6

Layout 6 features two operators, two trains, and two power sources or throttles. Running two trains in intersecting routes can be a test of skill and loads of fun. The two 90-degree crossings have to be modified to provide independent route capability (see page 71).

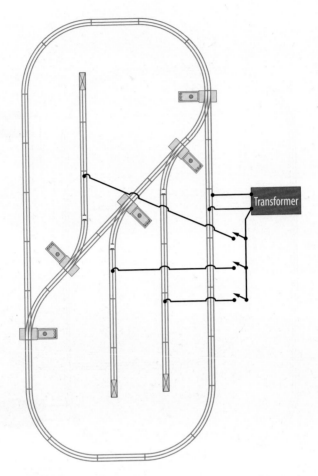

Layout 7

On Layout 7, one operator can run one train or one
train and a switcher. Three independent switched
spur sidings provide space for car loading and
storage. The basic track wiring is shown here. All
circuits are grounded through the running rails. For
clarity, the wiring of feeders, turnouts, and remote
control sections has been omitted.

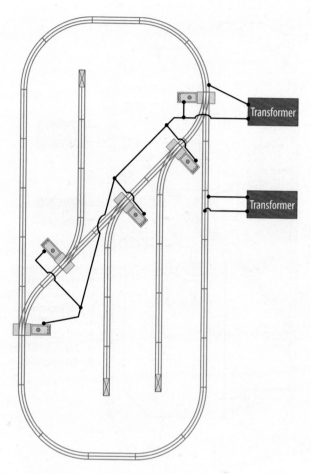

Layout 8

This layout shows how to wire a fixed-voltage power bus for the turnout motors. For positive action, 18 to 20 volts are recommended.

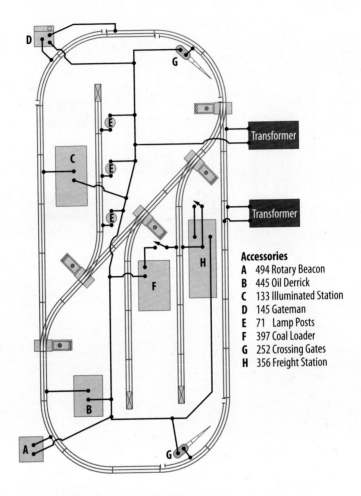

Accessories

A 494 Rotary Beacon
B 445 Oil Derrick
C 133 Illuminated Station
D 145 Gateman
E 71 Lamp Posts
F 397 Coal Loader
G 252 Crossing Gates
H 356 Freight Station

Layout 9

Layout 9 shows the wiring for a variety of postwar Lionel accessories. The fixed-voltage power bus is shown for lights and operating accessories, with 14 to 16 volts recommended.

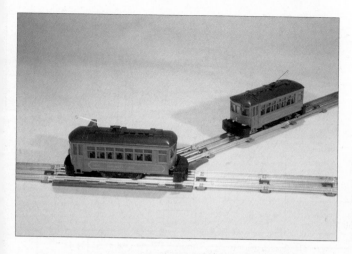

Using insulated track sections and a pair of turnouts, trolley cars can control themselves on a layout.

Completely automatic two-trolley line with station stops

Lionel's four-wheel Birney trolley cars have long been popular with operators. Designed to automatically reverse themselves upon impact with track bumpers, these little cars provide continuous point-to-point background activity. However, watching one car trek predictably between the bumpers soon becomes monotonous. It is easy to add operational variety to your layout with these trolleys. The station stop capability means more action than just bump-and-go.

This layout provides a new setting for them. It is completely automatic, requiring no attention from the operator, once it is set in motion. It features two trolley cars that make a number of stops on a small O-27 "waterwings" style layout. To make it more interesting, there's a stretch of single track between the loops that the cars must share, while moving in both directions.

The concept is quite simple and can be set up using specially insulated track sections and a pair of O-27 non-derailing turnouts. The two trolley cars will literally control themselves, automatically stopping and starting while throwing turnouts for the correct route. And it is accomplished without complicated wiring or relays.

As the diagram on the next page indicates, the layout has a continuous hot center rail with two insulated running rails at the stop sections and one insulated running rail at the trip sections. When the moving trolley car goes over a trip section, contact is made through the axles, and power is transmitted by wire to the appropriate stop section, which starts the other car.

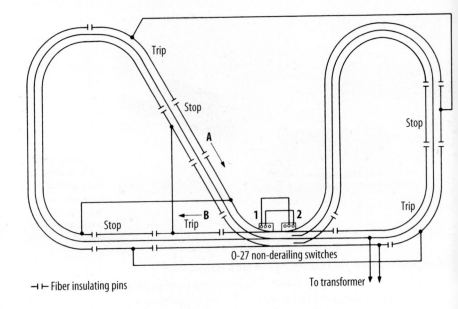

The operation cycle begins with cars at points A and B on the layout. Since stop sections immediately follow trip sections, there is little danger of collision. The additional current drawn when both cars are in motion adds to the realism by giving the impression of acceleration and braking.

The O-27 non-derailing turnouts are wired in tandem. As a result, they are simultaneously thrown for the correct route. When number 1 is thrown to red (the curved route), number 2 is thrown to green (the straight route), and vice versa.

More stops may be added to the line, but always in an odd number. Because the trolley cars are short, the stops do not need to be more than one track section in length. The trips should be at least two sections long. For optimum performance, you will probably have to experiment with various transformer settings.

The stop sections are easy to make. Insert four insulating pins into the running rails at both ends of the track section.

The trip sections have to be fabricated. The key is in isolating one running rail, using the fiber insulators from discarded pieces of track. Since the trips have to be two track sections in length, a steel pin is inserted in the middle and insulating pins at both ends of the insulated running rail.

Glossary

Alternating current (AC): Its flow of current rapidly alternates in direction many times per second. O gauge toy trains operate on this type of power.

Amperage: Unit of electrical measure that indicates the flow capacity of the system.

Block: A zone of control used when running two trains. It is an insulated stretch of track connected to its own On/Off switch or to a separate transformer throttle.

Circuit: Flow of electrical current that begins at the power source, travels to the object to be electrified, and returns to the power source.

Circuit breaker: Safety device that protects a transformer from burning out.

Coil: Wire wound around an iron core. In a transformer, the primary coil induces a weaker electrical field in the secondary coil to reduce voltage to a safe level.

Common ground: Wire that serves as a ground from track blocks, lights, or accessories on return to the power source.

Contactor: Contact-plate or spring-loaded switch that fits under track to operate train-activated accessories.

Direct current (DC): A relatively steady flow of current in only one direction, usually expressed as flowing from positive to negative in a circuit.

DPDT: A double-pole, double-throw switch can direct current from two separate circuits along two of four different paths. Some have an Off position between the poles.

DPST: A double-pole, single-throw switch is an On/Off switch that handles the power from two separate circuits.

Ground: Return leg or negative side of a circuit.

Ohm: Unit of electrical measure that indicates resistance.

Phasing: Linking two or more transformers on a layout by plugging all transformer cords into electrical outlets the same way, so trains pass smoothly from one insulated block to another.

Pole: Contacts on a switch.

Rectifier: Device used to convert AC current to DC.

Relay: An electromagnet having a movable iron armature attached to it, with one or more electrical contacts on the armature.

Rheostat: Device that adjusts resistance to control current.

Running rail: Outer rails of three-rail track.

Short circuit: When the flow of current takes a shortcut and returns to the power source and bypasses the electrical device it was intended to power.

Solenoid: Similar to an electromagnet but with its coil wrapped around a hollow, nonmagnetic tube with a movable inside.

SPDT: A single-pole, double-throw switch directs current along one of two separate paths. Some have an Off position between the two poles.

SPST: A single-pole, single-throw switch is a basic On/Off switch.

Switch: Electrical device that directs current along a path or shuts it on or off.

Throttle: Speed control on a transformer, operates by controlling resistance.

Toggle switch: Manual switch thrown with a handle.

Track pin: Metal connector between two pieces of track. Fiber or plastic pins are used to insulate track.

Transformer: Uses induction to reduce voltage from house current of 115 volts to a safe 18-20 volts for train operation.

Turnout: Track section that can move a train to another route.

UCS remote control track: Remote control sections that uncouple and unload train cars.

Voltage: Unit of electrical measure that indicates the force of the electricity.

Index

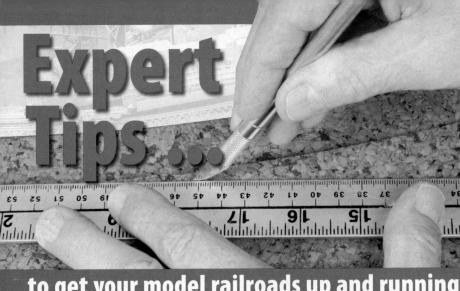

Expert Tips ...

to get your model railroads up and running

You'll find 16 realistic, themed layout plans, each including track diagrams, wiring schemes, and a list of suggested equipment in this book.
10-8350 • $18.95

Features layout descriptions, track requirements, operating suggestio and track plans for layouts that will fit bedroom to baseme sized space.
10-8275 • $15.95

Includes techniques and steps for lubrication, troubleshooting, and the right way to replace tires, batteries, and light bulbs.
10-8327 • $17.95

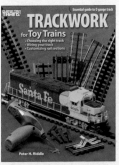

Provides an overvie of the various lines of sectional and flexible track, and demonstrates how cut, bend, wire, and install track int your layouts.
10-8365 • $19.95